STOLEN WATER, FORGOTTEN LIBERTIES
A True Story of Life Along Arkansas' South Highway 14 and the Buffalo River
©2014 Jenny Barnes Butler

Published by Hellgate Press
(An imprint of L&R Publishing, LLC)

Hellgate Press
PO Box 3531
Ashland, OR 97520
email: sales@hellgatepress.com

Editor: Harley B. Patrick
Interior design: Michael Campbell
Cover design: L. Redding

ISBN: 978-1555718046

Library of Congress Cataloging-in-Publication Data available from the publisher by request.

Printed and bound in the United States of America
First edition 10 9 8 7 6 5 4 3 2 1

Medicine for the Soul

STOLEN WATER, FORGOTTEN LIBERTIES

*A True Story of Life Along
Arkansas' South Highway 14
and the Buffalo River*

❧

JENNY BARNES BUTLER

Jenny Barnes Butler July 21, 21

Dedicated to Rena and Alice,
and all the women who know…
and yet, never give up.

Contents

Introduction

I AM NERVOUS. I simply cannot be in a hurry to tell this story. Sometimes I hurry out of fear—fear that I'll forget a detail or get distracted. I want to breathe and let this story flow. It's a simple story of a common man and a common woman who together lived remarkable lives. And, it's true.

I know for sure that stories are powerful and necessary. And while truth does not need to be proven again, there's always room for one more story. One more story to give someone else hope and a crack of light that energizes them to take one more step. I've chosen to tell this story using significant events that spotlight the development and depth of character of Joe and Willodean (nicknamed "Bill") Barnes. Few would have been able to shape such defeat, hardship, dysfunction, disappointment, and poverty into wealth. Not material wealth necessarily, but life riches. They did.

I am a daughter who wants to tell the story of these two dreadfully poor people, who, with no advantages or support, fell in love and lived irresistibly rich lives. I want the story of Joe and Bill to be enjoyed by their loved ones left behind and added to the memories cherished by all and included wherever God stores stories for our delight in eternity. Then we won't have to sit around and try to remember because we have this story in black and white. We can read it and laugh and cry and add more details and events as we recall more in heaven. One lifetime was not enough for these two.

When I was twirling a Hula Hoop around my waist for hours in the yard under the giant oak tree in front of what is now Wild Bill's Outfitters (located on South Highway 14 two miles from the Buffalo River in Marion County, Arkansas) I never dreamed or imagined I was the daughter of anyone unusual. I had what is often called a love/hate relationship with my father. I hated the way he treated my sister Shirley, and I was scared of him when he was drinking. But I loved how he loved me.I loved his physical strength, and I loved how people respected and listened to him. I loved how he commanded whatever situation he was in. Even then I was in awe of how my mother loved him.

Growing up I never gave much thought to the place we lived, other than there was absolutely nothing to do living so far out in the country, fourteen miles south of Yellville on Highway 14. Nothing to do but go to the river, or walk to my Grandmother Alice's house, half a mile north on 14, where I'd sit on the porch swing with her, drinking sweet tea and listening to her stories and views on life, which actually, looking back, was Academy-Award-like entertainment. She recited poetry, ballads, scripture, songs; she knew history and loved life. In the summers, my sisters and I were always on the lookout for a *True Story* magazine. I read all of Nancy Drew's books and *The Diary of a Young Girl* no telling how many times. Now I see what a gift the

Buffalo was to the whole community, without which southern Marion County would have been a wasteland of rolling Ozark hills covered with dusty apple-size rocks, plus back road after back road of billowing dust or sticky red clay mud, depending on the weather.

But the Buffalo gave us life. She birthed good and bad for many. Jimmy and Paul Ray Dillard (from the Dillard family who grew up on the river) would sit on a bluff near Tie Chute Hole with guns waiting to toy and torment fishermen as they floated down. No telling what else they did. At South Maumee, where pioneers settling close by crossed the Buffalo to get to Marshall, a young mother drowned as she was swept out of the family wagon away from her children as they crossed during high water. My older sister Shirley saved my younger sister Justine as she panicked trying to swim to the center of the river where the trusty refuge boulder waited.

The Buffalo gave us a respite. A place to be still and let go and remember what is important and what is not. She fed us the best catfish and bass, entertained us, and gave us an altar to worship. She shaped our lives as we floated, fished, trot lined, canoed, swam, made out with boyfriends, sang, played music, wrote songs and poetry, sat around campfires, hauled canoes, worked on guided fishing trips, and dreamed dreams. She gave us a hand to part the ice blue clouds and see the face of the creator. The Buffalo River connected the community, and for years on the lower forty miles of the river, Joe and Willodean Barnes, two nobodies from nowhere, made a difference.

In 1972 the Buffalo became the first designated "national river" after years of fighting between different factions. Some wanted to dam it in two places: the first one being above Lone Rock a few miles up from where it runs into the White River; the second place above Gilbert. Others wanted it to become government property so they could protect it and manage it. Then, some wanted everyone to just leave it alone and let the landowners take care of it the way they had for years. Much has already been written about the different factions and groups that grew out of this battle.

However, this is not a story about the battle over the Buffalo becoming a national river. This is a story that has never been told. The river and what happened to the land along it is the showcase that holds the account of Joe Barnes, an uneducated but colorful, damaged but commanding, leader in a community at a time when he was the one others trusted. He was the one people came to for answers. He knew what would work and what wouldn't. And, he was swayed by no one and nothing except by what was right. He knew that he would lose the battle to keep the river from becoming government held, but that didn't stop him from fighting with the other canoe operators along the river for the freedom to control their own livelihood through their businesses and their own property. This situation was virgin territory for the government. Always before, when they took land for parks and controlled the businesses, they owned the land where the business was. Not so in this case. They would be regulating businesses off government property.

When the Department of the Interior took over all the land along the 135-mile river (except Gilbert, which was incorporated as a city) in 1972, it took years for them to settle with the property owners. They started at the headwaters and worked their way down, negotiating and forcing people to sell. Next, they began to regulate who could be on the river, who could have a business using the river, and the rules and regulations they would have to follow.

In November of 1978, forty-four Buffalo River canoe operators received a letter in the mail informing them of a date for a meeting in Harrison to discuss how they could apply for a permit if they wanted to continue using the Buffalo.

"The world breaks everyone and afterward many are strong at the broken places," Ernest Hemingway writes in *A Farewell To Arms*. "But those that will not break it kills. It kills the very good and the very gentle and the very brave impartially. If you are none of these you can be sure it will kill you too but there will be no special hurry." Joe Barnes's destiny was one of struggle his whole life; unlike many he became stronger in the broken places. He made a difference.

This is his story. He did not write down anything, except how much money he had and where he left it. But he told me stories and I wrote them down. He told me about Rena, his mother, and called her "an orphan." He told me about his father losing his farm because he couldn't pay the $500.00 note due at the bank. He told me about meeting the beautiful Willodean and walking to Marshall to buy her a wedding dress. He told me about the Battle of St. Lo and going for ninety days without changing clothes when he was in France in WWII. I wrote his stories down, knowing I'd someday use them. He once told me after he read *Lonesome Dove*: "I don't know why someone in our family don't write a damn book." He thought we were educated idiots, for the most part, I suppose. All four of his girls graduated from college; three have master's degrees. Sure, he was proud of his girls and their educations, but "An education does not a smart person make," he was quick to relay.

Over the years, I kept hearing Joe's voice in my head and it had to come out the way I heard it. For that reason, the first and the last two chapters of this story are in Joe's voice, the way he said things, the way I wrote his stories down, the way I heard him speak. The Buffalo River gave Joe Barnes a place to leave a legacy few men have.

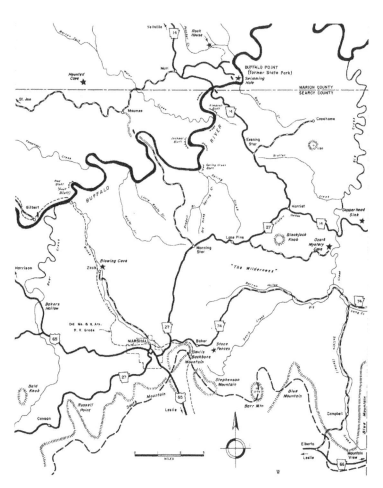

Buffalo River from Gilbert to State Park
(Reprinted with permission)

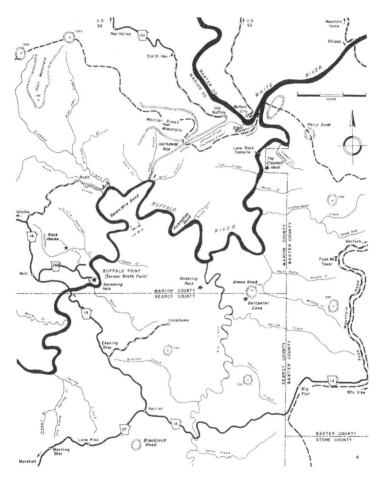

Buffalo River from State Park to White River
(Reprinted with permission)

Chapter One

A CANOE RENTAL AT HIGHWAY 14 BRIDGE

(IN THE WORDS OF JOE BARNES)

I BOUGHT THIS HERE LAND under the bridge in 1969. A man named Mr. Davis from Alaska come in here and started rentin' a few canoes and boats to people who didn't have 'em. He'd bought the land from Pate Dillard, who built and ran the ferry across the Buffalo before the bridge was built. Then Ira, Pate's brother, ran the ferry for years, chargin' fifty cents a car. They's a lot of history right here at this bridge. Stuff people ain't he'rd.

The land came with eleven old canoes, four leaky johnboats and four old good-for-not-much cabins. I didn't know if I could run a business. Never had run a business. Didn't know if I'd like it. 'Course I'd done a lot I hadn't liked. 'Bout all I knew was I was sick and tar'd of bein' away from Bill and the girls and livin' away from home. Tar'd a livin' in one room, boardin' in other people's homes while workin' on a lock or a dam for a few months.

I'd been runnin' around all over this United States workin' on locks and dams, from the St. Lawrence

Seaway to the Arkansas River system of locks and dams. The first dam I worked on was Bull Shoals, not long after I came home from the war. I didn't know much of anythin' 'bout carpenter work then. Knew so little I jest quit one day when the boss told me to go build a couple saw horses. Never forgit that day. I could hammer a nail, 'bout all I could do. Hadn't been there long when the boss jest up and said, "Joe go build us a couple saw horses so we can work on these forms over here." I was pretty bumfuzzled over that, but I tried and tried...then got mad and frustrated, exploded, threw down my hammer. Ended up jest leavin', packed up my stuff and jest left, quit and went home.

Once I got home, I couldn't rest. I drew some saw horses on a sheet of paper, got my tools out and it weren't long 'til I had cobbled out some semblance of saw horses. They weren't very purty. Few days later, I decided to load 'em on my truck and go see if they'd give me my job back. They hired me on the spot. I reckon they needed help bad or I was a fast learner and they wanted to keep me. Maybe both. Carpenter work suited me. I could see in my mind a picture of how things was supposed to work. I liked drawin' it out. At night when I was home, I'd sit and figure in my head and scribble and draw and sketch it out on paper. I was slow—but I could do math and I liked comin' up with the answers. I went to my jobs early to git ready for the day's work and I'd stay late. It weren't long 'til I moved up the ladder from carpenter to runnin' a crew as a foreman and then they put me over crews as a superintendent. I'd have to take the blueprints home and see that we stuck with the plan. I made damn good money. But jobs didn't last forever and I'd git restless and move from one good job to another, thinkin' somehow it would pay better or last longer. Guess the grass always looked greener. Me and Bill both would git to missin' home. When I finished a job, off we'd go to a new town or a new state, or maybe back to South Highway 14 where our little cracker-box house always set and waited on us.

We moved four times the year Jenny was in the first grade. Hell, I don't even remember why. Bill and the girls didn't think that much 'bout it, I don't reckon. Jest did it. Guess I jest got restless again. Restless or frantic, always lookin' for somethin' better, maybe longer, or higher payin'. Guess I never got over bein' raised in the Depression when I saw Momma and Daddy exhausted, worried sick 'bout whether or not they's gonna be able to feed us five growin' boys. I was searchin' for somethin' safe, I reckon. The last dam I was on was the Lock at Dardanelle with the Arkansas Lock and Dam System—'bout 1968, I reckon.

I knew a little 'bout the Buffalo River. There wasn't too much to know, I reckon. Most of all I knew to be careful when she's on a rise and especially when campin' overnight on a gravel bar. If it rained much up stream, next mornin' you'd wake up floatin' down river, if you slept on a raft. It doesn't take long for the river to creep up the gravel bar and take over durin' a flood.

Jimmy Dillard, one of Bill's cousins, was a good one to trot line and fish the river. People used to tell he could catch a catfish with his bare hands. We'd tie a line on one side of the river like we was puttin' up a clothesline and then drop shorter lines off it with hooks at the end, 'bout eighteen inches long or so every two feet. We'd bait each drop line as we stretched the main trot line all the way across the river.

Seinin' the river for bait was half the fun. Usually did that the night before and would have minnow buckets full of crawdads, perch, minnows, whatever we could use as live bait. Stink bait worked good too. Had to use anchors, like big heavy rocks to keep the lines under water after they were baited. Also kept big fish from runnin' off with the whole shebang. We'd git all this done right before dark and then sleep on the river bank. We'd tie cow bells ever 6 feet or so on the line. When we he'rd the bells ringin', we knew we had a fish. We'd be up, off an on, all night runnin' them lines, takin' the fish or snakes or eels off the lines and rebaitin' them. We'd catch a tub full of catfish!

Naturally, I was leery of runnin' a business since I hadn't ever run anythin' near like it before. A crew of carpenters is 'bout it. I was sure my ways weren't real well suited to customer service. Hell, I knew I was barely educated. A'int no dummy either. I can tell you one thing, by God, I'm a hell of a lot smarter than a lot of college graduates I've known. I was not known as a patient man either, to put it simply. And, to be honest, I knew I had a drinkin' problem that could interfere with business. 'Bout the only time I talked 'bout the drinkin' was when Bill and I had a blowup after I'd been on a binge. I'd go for months without touchin' a thing, then I'd git down an out and find somethin' to drink and then I had a hard time stoppin'. Comin' off a binge is a terrible feelin'. Damn!

We'd built Bill's grocery store in 1959, a mile up the hill from the bridge. It made damn good money for Marion County. I figured I could come out okay too—if I worked hard and put everythin' back in the business. I did know you can't spend your profit and makin' it would take hard work. 'Bout all I ever knew was hard work.

I hated to go in debt and I was stallin' 'bout buyin' at first. Bill insisted. "The land alone is worth what they are askin'," she kept sayin'.

"But, everything we have is paid for!" I argued back, "Our forty acres on top of the hill, the cracker box house, the store, vehicles, and even a little money stashed away." But she won. I bought early in 1969, like I said. I was tar'd of leavin' home. Besides, if Bill was for it, that meant a lot to me. She had a lot of sense, common sense.

I'm tellin' you my first spring and summer rentin' canoes and johnboats I could hardly keep up. That's the damn truth! I saw right away overnight guided trips was gonna be the money makers. You start addin' up the boat, motor, guide, food, tents, sleepin' bags, fishin' supplies, times the number of people and it adds up fast. But tourists who want a relaxin' few days away from city life were willin' to pay. Didn't take long for news to travel by word of mouth that we were the place to go for guided trips.

If a customer wanted to catch a fish, I had to have a good guide. Lots of good food and a comfortable dry bed at night on the river bank helped, but a good guide could make or break any trip.

The best guide I ever knew of on the Buffalo was a man named Robert Baysinger. Ole Robert was known as quite the "mountain man." He was quiet spoken and a nice appearin' man. He could catch a fish any-where, anytime, anyplace.

"There's a difference in a Yellow Cat and a Channel Catfish," Robert claimed. "A Yellow Cat has a home—under and around rocks and boulders. His tail sweeps them clean of brush and film so the rocks'll be nice and smooth—sometimes shiny." Seemed like he knew the fish like they was his family. I'm a tellin' you the truth.

Robert was raised on the lower end of the river. His dad, Ike Baysinger, was a logger and a farmer. He raised a lot of corn in a big field above the Highway 14 Bridge, between where Water Creek runs into the Buffalo and farther up, a place locals call Tie Chute Hole. I don't have any idée how far Robert went in school. He was smart and strong built. His kin was a pretty rough bunch of folk, I've he'rd. Moonshine business made you purty tough. Robert had a purty sister, Imogene, who married a cousin of Bill's, Paul Ray Dillard, from the Dillard bunch of Doc and Lizzie. Paul Ray was Jimmy's brother. His daddy was Ira, who run the ferry back n forth across the river. Their mother Meta was the tightest woman I ever he'rd of—she was so tight she rationed their food. Jimmy was a mean son of a bitch, I'ma tellin' ya and strong as a bull. I he'rd he ended up in California. Someone found him dead in a ditch out there. All these guys raised up fishin' on the Buffalo. They did lots of giggin' and trot linin' and spotlightin', not jest fishin'. Hell, these boys didn't grow up playin' baseball; they grew up on the Buffalo.

I had other good guides besides Robert in those early years of Buffalo River Fishing Resort. Jim Ward, who had 14 kids, worked for me for years. Bill worried herself sick 'bout those kids havin' e'nuff warm clothes and food. They lived down here in Big Bell Holler down on the park road on the other side of Dirst. Jim's wife, Donna, was a full blood Indian.

Jackie and Jimmy Morison were brothers from Marshall. Lord, what a pair those two were. Jimmy was with me one time we rescued a woman up the river in a terrible rainstorm. She was stuck, her legs trapped under the canoe seat when it folded like aluminum foil wrappin' around a tree. Water was up to her chin when we found her. 'Bout didn't git her out. Bill always wanted me to write that story and send it to *Reader's Digest*. Hell, I can't write. I can tell a story, but I can't write it. Remember I quit school in 'bout the fourth grade. Taught myself to read and write. She's the book smart one. She should'a wrote it.

Jackie didn't drink and didn't like to be round anyone who did drink. He's a fine guy. Hardworkin'. Honest. Danny Earl Tilley was from over across the river near or in the Nat'l Forest somewhere. Big guy, like a mountain man. Gary and Nancy Doskel worked for me cleanin' cabins and doin' office work and jest whatever needed to be done. They all was good help. I was lucky to have em. They were dependable. I had one woman worked for me who only had a few teeth. Can't remember her name. Hard worker, and clean but jest looked bad without many teeth.

I was keepin' ole Matt, my grandson, one weekend down at the bridge. Not sure where his momma, Jenny, was. Matt loved it at the bridge. Hell, all kids loved it down there. Who wouldn't? I jest let him go, runnin' free and wild. Told him not to go past his knees in the water without me with him. He minded pretty good— he wasn't much over three or four. I was sittin' on the porch with my cleanin' lady that Saturday, late in the afternoon. She was eatin' a tall Eskimo Pie. Matt walked up from the river and stood at the edge of the porch starin' at that ice cream. Before I could go buy him one, she stuck hers toward him to share it with him. He took a big lick and ice cream dripped off his chin. She took a lick, and offered him another lick. He licked again. Damn! I thought I'd die watchin' him lickin' off her ice cream. It didn't kill him, but it 'bout killed me.

My help was dependable. They weren't no college graduates. They knew how to work and appreciated the work. They weren't too goody good to git their hands dirty or stay late or pick up someone else's trash. I reckon I was the one that gave me the most trouble. I jest got to wantin' a drink ever once in a while, that burnin' sensation floodin' my veins triggered me not carin' 'bout much—wasn't much rhyme or reason to the way I drank. Some days I started early and drank a little all day. Some evenin's I drank straight vodka and tried to drink away the aches and emptiness. Some mornin's I felt rough, I can tell you for sure. I looked rough too. But, the show went on. Customers wanted to float. They tolerated the rough way I'd look, a beard, clothes been slept in. My help stepped in and picked up the slack. Didn't seem to hurt business, but back then there weren't that many places to rent a canoe. Hard to be too picky. But people absolutely began to flock to the Buffalo. I never seen anythin' like it.

The battle over the Buffalo was in the news 'bout ever damn day, seemed like. Always some new somethin' abrewin' 'bout whether to dam it or make it a Nat'l River. People in little groups fightin' over it like it was their only child someone tryin' to kidnap.

Prob'ly, the best way to 'splain the battle is this: They was two main groups of people. One was the tree huggers who wanted the gov'ment to step in and make the river like a national park all the way up and down the 135-mile river along with the land on either side and the gov'ment control it all to protect it. Most locals didn't want the damn gov'ment comin' in here tellin' us what we could and couldn't do with our land. Most locals that is.

Over round Marshall it was a different story. They wanted a dam above Gilbert 'cause a dam would bring in more tourists and mean more business for them, like it is over at Bull Shoals Lake since they dammed the White River. These pro-dam folks organized earlier in 'bout 1962 and formed the Buffalo River Improvement Association (BRIA). They was jest a group of business folks who saw the commercial benefits over round Marshall that wanted both dams—the one at Lone Rock above the mouth of the Buffalo three or four miles and the one right above Gilbert. They was pushin' and arguin' the dams would help with electrical power, water conservation and help with tourism and industry. They were okay with a national river but wanted it upstream from the Gilbert dam. I reckon the tree huggin' group decided they didn't want no half a river. They kept fightin' for the whole river to be made national river.

I been told the first meetin' between the two in this war was called by the Corps of Engineers in Marshall early in 1962—the outcome was a clear victory for the pro-dam folks. But I he'rd that was when Neil Compton's bunch figured out theys gonna havta git busy.

Then, in April of that same year, Supreme Court Justice William O. Douglas floated the Buffalo for several days with a group of dam opponents. Afterwards, he became vocal 'bout his favorin' the preservation of the river as a national river. He was quoted as sayin', "This river is too beautiful to die."

A month or so after Douglas's visit, other preservation proponents, who knew 'bout the BRIA recent meetin' in Marshall and pickin' up steam, gathered at the University of Arkansas campus and ended up establishin' the Ozark Society headed up by Dr. Neil Compton and Mrs. Laird Archer. Their objective was "the preservation of the Buffalo River and adjacent areas in their natural state." Anyway, that's what I he'rd.

A course I was still roamin' all over the country then 'bout 1962. So I've jest read and he'rd 'bout some of these doings. But then, after I bought in 1969, it weren't but a couple years 'til I could hardly keep up with my business. I jest kept buyin' more canoes and more vans and trucks and trailers to haul them in. Hirin' more people to work. Ever canoe would be rented on weekends we had decent weather.

Local and national news coverage of the battle over the Buffalo made people curious what all the fuss was 'bout, I reckon. Newspapers, magazines and TV all seemed to follow the story. We had people comin' in here from 'bout every state in the United States.

I knew, a course, 'bout the battle to make it a national river when I bought, but no one really knew how it would fall for sure. I mostly jest wanted them all to go home and leave us the hell alone. I reckoned it would happen sometime though. The gov'ment wasn't gonna jest let the river be.

Seemed like the fight was goin' to go on forever. David Pryor (senator from Arkansas 1979-1997) came and wanted me to show him the river and how all the canoe haulers worked. So did Faubus (governor of Arkansas, 1955-1967).

Like I said, business was good. People came in here from all over to float the Buffalo, city slickers, rich, poor. Lots of businesses brought groups of their people, like the Arkansas Razorback football team, the Case Knife Company. Some knew how to paddle. Some didn't. Some would, honest to God, git in a canoe, and start paddlin' up the river. Damn! Can you imagine? I'm a tellin' you the truth.

But people came from Louisiana, Mississippi, and a lot from Texas. Some stayed, camped out for months in the park and here at my place in the summer. Some customers would not do a damn thing I told 'em to do. Others couldn't do e'nuf for you—when it came to takin' care of canoes, paddles and all like they was their own.

Runnin' the business became long hours and hard work. Durin' the canoein' season, April, May, June, July, August and September, I'd sleep in my office buildin' next to the bridge on the weekends. Customers called or stopped by all hours of the day and night. If I was here, I didn't miss any business. I knew to make hay while the sun shined. I kept the good-for-not-much cabins clean and they stayed rented. Families came to vacation or spend a day swimmin' in the river, picnickin' or jest playin'. Others wanted long, serious overnight, fishin' trips. Bill used to say regularly, "My myyyyy—HOW people love that river—-should be a song." Damn.

I reckon I took on a different kind of way dealin' with customers. Some people have said a "style." Basically, I didn't take any shit off no one. But, I tried hard to give people their money's worth and see to it they was safe on the river and had a chance to have fun. Some things I jest could not tolerate.

Makin exceptions for people is one of 'em and waitin' on people is another. If I told a person the time to git picked up after a float was four o'clock, by God I meant four o'clock. I ain't waitin' round an hour while they deedaddle around and play and take their good ole pokey time gittin' there. Rules are rules, by God and I'll run my business the way I want. If someone don't like it they can go somewheres else and rent a damn canoe. Fine with me.

The first time Mike Mills came to visit the lower end of the Buffalo, I was standin' outside on the porch talkin' to a new customer. I usually wore blue jeans, cowboy boots, a white shirt, and a ball cap cocked to one side. That's jest what I was comfortable in and it washed good. Haulin' canoes can be dirty work. The customer and Mike reached the porch at 'bout the same time.

"Are you Mr. Barnes?

"That's me," I told him.

"Can we rent a canoe and float down the river from here?"

"Sure can. You can put in here and float down to the state park, take you 'bout an hour, or you can go on to Rush, 'bout a ten mile float, five or six hours, depends on how fast you paddle. We will have a truck there to pick you up and bring you back to your car. Jest up to you on how long you want to be on the river."

Well, they hum hawed around, talked 'bout food, tryin' to decide what to do. All the while Mike was waitin' on 'em, tryin' not to butt in.

"How will we know where to take out of the water?" they asked.

"They's a big iron cable stretched high from one side of the river to another, right before you git to Rush. Used to be a cable car that crossed there when Rush was a boomin' zinc mine town."

"What do we do if your driver and truck aren't there?"

"My driver will be there," I told 'em, losin' my patience.

"What if we aren't there yet by 4 o'clock?" he asked.

"By God, if you aren't there by 4 o'clock, you'll have to walk the ten miles back to your car," I told 'em and finished that conversation.

Later, ole Mike told me that day he knew he'd found a style of dealin' with customers. Kinda funny, I reckon. Mike had been in graduate school at Fayetteville when he first floated the Buffalo and fell in love with it. Soon he dropped out and bought the canoe business at Ponca and changed the business' name to Buffalo Outdoor Center.

I've he'rd Mike tells this story on me. Uses it as a model for how he wanted to deal with people and run his business.

A few years after the law passed makin' it a national river in 1972, but before the government takeover of our land, seemed like they was always somethin' excitin' or important happenin' at the river. River was floodin'. River was too low to float without draggin' a canoe, dryin' up from no rain. Someone drownin' in an accident, a car wreck on the river hill. People was riled up over the government forcin' us to sell our land and not jest that but them takin' over and tellin' us what we could do and what we couldn't do. Most of all, forcin' us to move off our land along the river. People who'd had this land in their family for generations.

Weren't never dull around here for long with Bill runnin' the grocery store and all that bunch of her family, the Smiths comin' around and then there's all the Dillards too. Frankly, I never cared much for hullabaloo, but didn't have no choice lots of the time. Winters was slow, but early in the year, people started callin' and bookin' trips, cabins, canoes. I kept a poster size, homemade, calendar beside my recliner in the livin' room to schedule for cabins and float trips and canoes. Early, in March I believe, 1976, the *National Geographic* Society contacted me 'bout one of their people comin' to float the Buffalo. They wanted to canoe the total 135 miles of the river and they would write up a story for the magazine. I reckon everyone knew 'bout *National Geographic*. Right away, I perked up and knew this would be an important story for the river, all of us canoe haulers and businesses up and down it.

The canoe haulers, U.D. Lynch, Leon Dodd, Dirst and Joe Bennet, didn't max out their capacity or rent all their canoes very often, exceptin' for holiday weekends like Memorial Day, the 4th of July or Labor Day. This set me to figurin', means I went to my recliner, looked at my calendar, startin' circlin' my thumbs with balls of fingers on each hand, chewin' tobacco. I'd stretch out my size twelve cowboy boots, legs stickin' straight out from my recliner, leanin' back, in meditatin' position.

Called 'em back. Told 'em I could handle from Pruitt down to the mouth. I didn't want any part of Ponca to Pruitt, which can be pretty treacherous in the spring if they's high water. They was other good outfitters up there knew better what was goin' on up there. They could keep floaters safe and informed of the river levels and the weather. Hell, Ponca is 100 miles or more up the river from me. Can be lots of white water up there in April when we'd be makin' this trip. Can't remember if Mike Mills had bought the place at Ponca yet or not. Believe he had.

National Geographic folks wanted a good guide and someone to handle the commissary boat. The guide would be the person who knew the river's twists and turns. He'd set up camp on a gravel bar, put up tents, cots, make a fire and either do the cookin' or help the cook if they'd hired one. He'd help them fish or do whatever they wanted.

"I'll git you the best guide ever been on this river," I told them. I set to figurin' how I'd git Robert Baysinger to make this trip. I'd he'rd some rumors recently 'bout a murder happened in Marshall, 'bout thirty miles away. Billy Joe Holder was the man's name. He worked for the Arkansas Beverage Control, but before that he'd been the youngest sheriff ever in Marshall for years. People seemed to either really like him or really hate him. I didn't know the man. His reputation was bein' a hardass on moonshiners and Marshall was a dry county. Holder was tough and held his ground. Somebody shot him late in January that year, I believe. People was sayin' Robert Baysinger was in on it.

Hell's bells, I didn't believe Robert Baysinger could shoot nobody. Jest couldn't believe it. Robert was a gentle soul, although he was a tough old coot too. He was backwoods, hill country, but he wasn't a murderer. He'd made moonshine for years. I'd drunk some of it. Last I'd seen him, he seemed pretty down and out 'bout it all, but as far as I knew no one had been arrested yet. And, I didn't believe it anyway. *National Geographic* wouldn't know 'bout these rumors. They jest needed a guide. I needed him. If I was goin' to give *National Geographic* the best trip they could git to be written down and recorded and read by many for years, it'd be a cryin' shame not to use Robert.

It was a cold March mornin'. I drank my coffee, pulled on my boots, got my hat and coat and left early to drive over to Harriett to find where Robert lived. I didn't call him. He'd be up. I didn't figure he'd been strayin' too far from home with all the rumors flyin' round 'bout the murder. People, even locals, might be leery of anyone in the bootleggin' circle, especially if the rumor is he may have shot the sheriff. Damn!

Turnin' off the paved highway onto the dirt road, I drove through the tree lined lane and shortly pulled my truck within a few yards of Robert's front porch. Not quite daylight, I saw a faint light inside and then saw movement by a curtain over the picture window. Standin' on Robert's front porch, I could see miles and miles of rollin' Ozark Mountains. A purty place. I knocked.

He opened the front door and motioned me inside. With a warm grin and outstretched hand, we shook while he pulled me inside. We drank coffee and shot the bull awhile. Then I told him why I come. "I got a big float trip comin' up for the *National Geographic* magazine," I told him. "It will give the river a lot of good attention and advertisement if we make it fun and safe." "By God, Robert, I told 'em I'd git the best guide ever was or ever will be on the Buffalo; you're that one."

"Now Robert, I know they's some serious rumors flyin' 'round 'bout you bein' involved in the Billy Joe Holder case, but I don't believe 'em for one single minute."

"Joe, what on earth people gonna thank 'bout you hiring a suspect in this case? What'll people say 'bout you and your business?" Tears rolled down his face.

"Robert, I don't give a DAMN what people say!"

National Geographic didn't publish the article for 'bout a year, March of '77. Course we all 'bout forgot all 'bout it by then. Here's how the journalist, Harvey Arden, started out:

> OUT IN THE DOWN-HOME HILLS of the Arkansas Ozarks runs a 135-mile wriggle of near wilderness that maps call the Buffalo River and local folks call just "Buf'lo." Kicking its white-water heels through sparsely populated hills as tough and worn as a farmer's overalls, this frisky calf of a stream—one of a dwindling number of un-

dammed rivers in the eastern half of the United States—was set aside by Congress in 1972 to run forever free as America's first officially designated "national river."

The pictures in the article are as good as any I ever seen, Hemmed-in-Holler, white water rapids, bluffs, Gilbert General Store, people in canoes, Granny Eva Barnes Henderson who at 83 years old had to move from home. When asked 'bout the new national river, which would make us owners have to move outside the park boundaries, she said, "Moving out o' here would mean giving up all I've got, all I ever had." She died less than a year after she was forced to move from her home. One other local person was mentioned and that was Fred Dirst at Rush who told them 'bout the zinc mines and the town when it was boomin'.

Was it a good story 'bout the Buffalo? Yes, I'm sure it was. Did it capture the flavor of what it's like to float? Maybe, maybe not. Did it give history and tell 'bout the battle over dammin' it or the government regulatin' it? Some. Did it reflect a poetic romance with the river? Seemed so.

Jest seemed like somethin' missin' to me, maybe like a description you'd hear of Disneyland—or some kind of fantasy. I didn't hear the heartbeat of the river like you did in the letter Faubus wrote askin' the river be left alone.

Robert tells his version of floating the Buffalo with the group of people including the *National Geographic* team:

> At Pruitt, I joined Mr. Arden, his wife, Lorraine, and their two children, six and three, and his sister-in-law, Mary Kimley, and her three children, ages fifteen, fourteen, and ten, after they'd been on the river two days coming down from Ponca.
>
> Seemed like all they brought to eat was what I call hippie food. They'd get out a bowl and add nuts and fruit and mix it all up. Joe Barnes was known for the good meals he provided on overnight trips. For one-night trips they were usually a big thick rib eye or a T-bone steak with baked potatoes, peaches on a bed of lettuce, and corn on the cob. But Joe hadn't provided food for this trip, just a guide. I guess after two days they'd run out of most meal stuff cause I couldn't look at no more of that hippie stuff. I needed some food! When we got close to the Highway 65 Bridge and took a break, I spotted some big rocks I thought might be hiding some catfish. I'd brought my Rouge gig. Wasn't long 'til I'd gigged two catfish around 5 pounds each. I cleaned them and put em in the cooler. Then, right around the bend was a game warden. His name was Darrell Tucker. We stopped and talked. He saw the fish and the gig but didn't say a word. I's sho'r proud of that.

I was a starving to death by the time we got to Gilbert. I left the boat on the gravel bar, walked up to the Gilbert General Store. I bought corn meal, potatoes and shortening. Later that night, when we made camp, I fried up that catfish, cooked fried potatoes and made golden brown hush puppies. No more hippie food for awhile. They wasn't one bite left over. Think they enjoyed something besides hippie food themselves.

A couple days later, further down the river, we got close to Rush. I was starting to get hungry for something hearty again and thought I'd try my hand at gathering up more food rather than suffer through the hippie menu. This time I caught a ten pound catfish in the Silver Holler Hole close to Rush. When I was getting ready to fry it, someone asked me if I had anything to go with it. We were out of potatoes. I started looking around and saw a nice patch of Poke Salad. I cut off the tops, chopped up the stalks, rolled 'em in corn meal and served another tasty meal on the river bank. No leftovers again.

The evenin' after this trip was over, Robert Baysinger and Leon Dodd spent the evenin' at Robert's house drinkin' and shootin' the bull. The next mornin', a sheriff from Marshall knocked on Robert's door and arrested him for the murder of Billy Joe Holder. Another story. A longer story.

After the government forced me to sell my property at the bridge, I moved my business on top of the river hill. That was in 1980. Robert had been in the pen 'bout a year. After a retrial, he was released. His earlier conviction was overturned. Another story. But after awhile, he started workin' for me again. He worked in the office answerin' the phone some, hauled canoes, and still guided on fishin' overnight trips. Bill worked across the road. She kept a close eye on me then. I was still bad to drink. I know I was. I wish I could take it back but I can't. At times I'd git mean. Nothin' would make me stop lookin' for a fight.

She would call up at the canoe office and ask for Robert. She thought he'd tell her the truth. "Is Joe a drinking today?" she'd ask. Robert would say somethin' like, "He may have had a beer or two." He never told her too much detail.

After a big rain, the river would rise and turn muddy and flood. When I could see we were fixin' to lose every single rental of the 165 canoes I now had, I'd send someone to Cotter for a case or two of beer, some Jack Daniels whiskey and tell Robert to git a johnboat ready.

We'd put a ten horse motor on the back of a boat, load it up and be sure we had a jacket of some kind. The river gits cool in the evenin's. Somethin' 'bout motorin' up that river—leavin' civilization—hearin' the hum of the motor, the boat cuttin' through the water, the splash of nature in my face that made me breathe deep and wonder if maybe I hadn't done somethin' good—somethin' worthwhile with the deck of cards God dealt me. I'm not sure. I did wonder.

Robert could be trusted to run the boat and motor, no matter how big the river flooded or how muddy or how many trees or cows were floatin' in it. Worries and troubles rolled off my back the further we motored up. I'd forgit all 'bout the $3,000 or $4,000 of business I was losin' that weekend and all my employees workin' for me losin' their pay when I had to send 'em home.

Yes I'd git sloppy drunk at times, but "I never seen him when he couldn't run his business," I overheard Robert tell someone. And, I always knew Robert wasn't goin' to "tattle" to Bill.

Chapter Two

GROWING UP IN INDEPENDENCE COUNTY

N ONE OF THE FEW PHOTOS of my father as a young man, he is standing tall on the roof of our little cracker-box house nestled at the fork of South Highway 14 and Highway 268 in the hills of southern Marion County, Arkansas. A hammer hangs down from his hand. Lean and muscular, he's wearing a white tank T-shirt and loose khakis. His legs, long like a granddaddy long-leg spider, and the cloudy sky above him, makes it look like he stretches all the way to heaven. He's wearing a Harrison Ford–type Fedora, tilted a bit to the left to cover his already balding head. Relaxing after roofing the house, he stands with his hand on his hip and his right knee bent. He looks strong.

Because our house did not have indoor plumbing, he would fill a five-gallon cream can from a spring the other side of my grandmother's, down the road about a mile, and carry it on his shoulders the mile back home. It's no wonder he made his girls share bath water. He couldn't afford to drill a well and there was no city water out that far from Yellville, the closest town.

"You ready, Jen?" Dad asked as he came out the front door of the house onto the gray cement front porch. It was late afternoon in the spring of 1950; the sky was cloudy and it was looking rainy. He lifted me up into the cab of the only vehicle he owned, a flatbed truck, and tucked me behind his shoulder. I was three years old, with blonde stringy hair and fat round cheeks. My left arm scooted tightly around his hairy, warm neck. I felt his joy in having me there beside him. I fit perfectly in the little secure wedge behind his muscular shoulder.

He began to sing as the truck coasted down the mile and a half grade of the Buffalo River hill:

> *Me and Ole Jen… Goin' down the road*
> *Just me an Ole Jen… Goin' down the road… together*
> *Ho! Ho! Ho!*
> *Just me and Ole Jen in my Ole Ford*
> *Ho! Ho! Ho!*
> *Just me and Ole Jen… in my Ole Ford… together*

He sang loudly. Over and over he'd repeat the verses. Over and over. He'd add something here and there to break it up, usually something silly like "over the hill and around the bend," with lots of ho, ho, ho's. He'd try to make it rhyme but it didn't matter if it didn't.

The heart of the song was that we were together, just the two of us, and I believe he loved it as much as I did.

The more he sang, the tighter I'd scoot in behind his shoulder, feeling secure and loved and very important. This is my earliest memory. He had a fresh, brisk woodsy smell with clothes of rough flannel or wool, like his whiskers. My mother, Mary Willodean, nicknamed "Bill," used to say, "Joe is the best-looking man I ever saw."

It started to rain as we hummed down South Highway 14 in that big old noisy truck and turned East at Harriet for what should have been a two-hour trip. His mother, Rena, had been sick, and Dad was good about visiting her after he'd returned from the war in 1945. He sent her an allotment out of his check the whole four years he was in the service. "Joe has very tender feelings toward his mother," Mom used to say. His mother lived in a tiny place called Magness, close to Newark, Arkansas.

I can't remember Grandma Rena as a young woman; to me she was an old lady with a neatly designed bun pulled tightly behind her head. As many women did in that era, she dipped snuff, a powdery tobacco, staining her teeth. They were small teeth, maybe worn down from wear, I suppose, looking as if she'd never lost her baby teeth. She wore print dresses, little print like the kind that used to be on flour sacks, and made her own clothes. Around the waist she added tiny pockets where she kept her money hidden and secure. Her life full of tragedy, I've always thought maybe her pain made her numb to joy as well as sadness, since her emotions were flat. Surely, a child knowing his mother had endured the hardships such as Rena had would make him feel tender toward her as Dad did. He always referred to Rena as an orphan.

When she was four months old, Rena was given to a man and woman named J.M. and Martha Finch. She did not know it, but she had an older brother and sister who were each given to different families. Rena's biological mother became ill when her husband left her with three children. Why he left, no one knows. She ended up in the sanatorium in Batesville, Arkansas, and may have never left. Although the spelling of Rena's mother's name was unclear, she was known as Anna Bowers. Rena, born in Moorefield on Valentine's Day, 1887, was not legally adopted until she was sixteen.

Rena was attractive when she was young. An old, worn picture clearly shows a tiny waist that gave her an hourglass figure, lovely brown hair pulled up and twisted back from her face, and brown eyes that twinkled. Her smile showed she was shy and hesitant, but proud. Her adoption papers say J.M. Finch "educated" her, but her handwriting shows she could barely write her own name, and J.M. signed his name with an "X." It's interesting that Martha Finch didn't sign the adoption papers, nor was she even mentioned. My father referred to them as "good people."

Since the Finches were farmers, Rena worked on the farm until meeting Joseph George Barnes. They married in 1911 and lived in Magness, where he worked at whatever was available including one job as a tool boy. He would go in after the miners quit for the day and gather up all the tools and carry them out. At age 11, he was trapped for three days because of a cave-in. After Rena and Joseph George got married, he worked at a gravel pit and then on the railroad until he began farming.

Their first child, Marguerite, born one year after they were married, lived only three months, as noted in Rena's Bible. Two years later, Rena gave birth to her first son, George, who lived six months. No one ever really spoke about why the babies died, and a third one died the day it was born and was never named. In 1916, Rena had her first child that lived to adulthood, James Lindsey. My father, Joseph William, was born three years later. Next came Jarrell Franklin, and then Jordan Robert, followed by the last son, Kenneth Kirby.

Mom said, "Rena never did like her daughters-in-law much." Mom thought Rena wanted her sons to herself, without the wives. Rena called my mother "trash" because she smoked. "Only trashy women smoke," Rena told Dad. And she asked him, "Why would you want to marry a woman that's trash?" Mom said this devastated her for a while as she'd never been called trash before.

Still, Rena's sons were thoughtful and affectionate toward her. Dad talked about what a grand cook she was and how she would bake wonderful pies and cakes when holidays came around. Her homemade mince-meat pie was his favorite. He said each year she used to can hundreds of cans of vegetables and also vegetable soup. Many times at breakfast all they'd have would be a half-gallon jar of her canned blackberries and a pan of her browned, hot "cat head" biscuits.

"I was about fourteen and remember that day well," Dad said. "We lived in the farmhouse outside Newark. Momma was in the kitchen as usual and there was a knock on the front door. A young man was standing there on the porch with a woman. He asked if they could come in. I let them in and called for Momma to come see these folks. The man asked if Rena Barnes lived there. When Momma came in the room, he told her his name was Frank Gibbs and he introduced the woman as Maggie James. He told her he was from Dallas, Texas, and Maggie lived only about fifteen miles down the road from us near Newark. Frank told Momma he was her brother and that Maggie was her sister. They sat around in the living room all morning talking and getting to know each other."

Rena was forty-six when she met her brother and sister. "I really liked them both," Dad recalled. He always looked forward to summertime after that because he said his Uncle Frank's wife was from Oil Trough and he visited them regularly. Dad lived one whole summer with Maggie, in fact, and worked on her farm. "She was nothing like Momma," Dad said.

"It wasn't long after that when the Depression hit and Daddy lost our farm," Dad said. "Cotton was selling for fifty cents a pound the year Daddy bought the farm." My grandfather, Joseph George, rented some land along with what he bought. He started with four head of horses and some mules. Later that year when it came time to sell what they had grown, cotton was bringing only ten cents a pound. It hadn't rained much, there had been a drought, and the crop was no good. When the note for the farm came due, they still owed $500.00 to the bank. They weren't able to make the payment. The bank would not extend the loan, and took the farm. The entire Barnes family—Rena, Joseph George, James, Joseph William, Jarrell, Jordan, and Kenneth—loaded up everything they could pack onto a horse-driven wagon and rode away from the house. Dad was fifteen. They had to find a rental house after that. Joe said, "I never in all my life saw such a look on a man's face as I saw on Daddy's face that day; he was never the same man after that."

Cruising along toward Rena's home, the roads were brown dirt, not paved then, most of the way from South Highway 14 to Newark. As it became darker, the rain came down harder, accompanied by thunder and lightning. We turned off the main road in Newark onto a narrow back road that would take us straight to Rena's house. It had been raining there a long time, as the road was already red, sticky clay mud, and shortly the truck tires were stuck deeply and would not move. We sat there a while waiting for it to quit raining, and Joe mumbled about what to do next. Finally, when the storm subsided, he turned to me and said, "Jen, I'm going to go get help and try to find some tire chains to get us out of this mess. You can't go with me. You'd get wet and you might get sick. Stay right here and Daddy will be back in a little while." He hugged me tight and kissed me, and then quickly left the cab of the truck. I turned and watched his back as he walked away into the thick black night. I didn't cry.

I stood in the cab of the truck with my nose pressed to the back window watching the liveliness of the storm. Since this had never happened before, I started to worry about him out in the dark by himself but never once feared that my father would not come back for me. Maybe I was a little scared, but not about his returning. This incident may have been the beginning of the way I worried about him much of my life. Later on, I worried because he didn't go to church and I didn't want him to go to hell. That's what the Church of Christ, where I went, taught. I always worried because he worked so hard and he didn't have a son or anyone to help him. He used to complain to Mom that all we girls thought about was what we were going to wear, and he'd say, "I just wish I had someone to help me do some work around here." I worried about his binge drinking. After a drinking spree of a few days when he was sobering up, he became remorseful and seemed so defeated. "I'm just a son of a bitch," he'd say, sitting with his head drooped into his hand, rubbing his forehead with his cap scooted back. I worried that he didn't like himself. I worried about how he treated my sister, Shirley, and how hateful he was to her at times. I would do anything to keep him from yelling at me or being critical. It pierced my heart when he'd say, "Well, why in the hell did you do that?" That wait in the truck when I was three colored the way I saw my father from then on in two important ways: It was the birth of me worrying about him and of me being secure in the belief that he would always be there to take care of me.

I watched and waited for his return for what seemed like forever. It rained more. It thundered, and occasionally the lightning would light up the sky and I could see down the road. Soon, I saw his black shape moving toward the truck carrying an armload of chains.

He had walked to someone's house and borrowed the chains. I watched as he worked in the red sticky mud to get them on the back tires. He worked and wrestled with them until finally they were secure. Soon we were on our way and I squeezed back behind that muscular shoulder.

Today when I think about Rena, I'm sorry I didn't get to talk to her and explore her past and ask her how she managed without a mother or a sister. Her home was a little weathered gray country house with a tiny porch. It smelled hot and stuffy. A bed was in the living room, a couch on the other side with a table and chair. The walls were wallpapered a simple flowery pattern. Old baby pictures of her sons, and then later some of their families, sat on a bookshelf next to where she sat and relaxed. "How've you been?" she'd ask grabbing my hands and shaking them, smiling up at me with her sawed-off looking teeth. She'd squint when she smiled. And sometimes the snuff would drip into the cracks of her smile. She wore no makeup, but was blessed with smooth, lovely skin. Still, I was afraid of her. She seemed mysterious and unknowable.

I have her Bible. Jordan gave it to me before he died. It looks like a book she treasured but didn't read very much. It has a plastic cover on it and few markings in it. It carries scribbled dates of family members' births, marriages and deaths. Old ragged pages of a previous Bible are taped in the middle. Her handwriting is large and unsightly. I wonder what she did with her grief.

Chapter Three

A COMMUNITY
ON SOUTH 14

I AM SIXTEEN. I have a date and he's late. It's black dark outside. As I look out the living room picture window, I see lights flicker in the distance as the car rounds a curve miles away. Shortly, he pulls up in the driveway. Where will we go for a date this late? It's fourteen miles back to Yellville and the only entertainment there is the Dairy Queen.

"Let's go to the river," I suggest. It's a warm summer night. We can wade the gravel bar and talk. No one else will be there. We drive two miles to the main swimming area in the park. Clear bright stars light the way down to the sand as we find a place to spread the blanket. We sit in the sand and listen to the stillness of the night and the river ripples. He clicks a Zippo lighter and offers me a cigarette. We smoke, then begin talking in a whisper as if not to interfere with the silky sounds of river movement. He kisses me.

In southern Marion County, Arkansas, life is connected to the Buffalo River, flowing 135 miles from first trickle and ending at the White River. Many tiny, one-lane dirt roads and much of rural life, such as fishing and Sunday picnics, lead to the warm gravel hemming the edge of the river's green water. Along the last thirty miles sits an entire community I call South Highway 14, with a little place called Mull at its center.

The first people to discover the area—Indians, trappers, pioneers, and fishermen—were drawn by the Buffalo and the many surrounding little streams feeding into it: Water Creek, Desoto Springs, Clabber Creek, Caney Creek, and Spring Creek. People naturally settled close to water no matter how rocky or hilly or hard the land. Mull sits two miles north up the mountain from the Buffalo, near the entrance to the main park that captivates people with breathtaking hilltop views, limestone bluffs, and sandy, gravel swimming areas along the river. From 1919 to 1944, Mull had a post office run first by my Aunt Mabel Dillard Davenport, and then taken over by her younger sister, my grandmother, Alice Dillard Smith.

Mull is not a town, has never been a town, and will never be a town. But it is central in the community with other places, Maumee and Rush, which had their heyday as booming mining towns in the early 1920s. Together they make up the community called South Highway 14 because that highway is the main artery leading to the river through the ghost towns of Rush and Maumee. Plus, that's what locals call the area.

My mother, Mary Willodean Smith, said when she was growing up she rarely, if ever, saw a car until her father, Harrison Smith, bought his first one, a 1926 Ford Model T, for $500.00. Her grandparents, Doc and Lizzie Dillard, were one of the first families to build a home in Mull. In the 1920s people traveled by walking or riding a horse or in a wagon, so it was quite a thrill for the Smiths to own a car. The car was started by turning the crank in the front. It must have been fairly light because when Doc accidentally ran over Bill's younger brother, Leroy, he was not hurt at all. Another time during a drive down the steep Caney Hill behind their home, Doc Smith lost control and the car turned over into the holler, but no one was hurt.

Bill, the oldest girl of nine children, always said she had wonderful Christian parents. But her mother, Alice, was often "sickly," and had been her entire life. Bill had to shoulder a big part of the household work, like caring for the babies that kept coming despite Bill's complaints. Her chores included cooking and cleaning without any modern conveniences, including no electricity. They cooked on a woodstove, and the family's water supply came from a cistern that held rain water.

Even though she was a poor country girl with few clothes, Bill was elegant. In every picture of her when she was young, she was poised like a model on a runway with silky coal black hair. She'd rest her wrist on her tiny waist, her left knee touching her right knee, and her foot slightly lifted off the ground with her chin thrown back high.

She declared she paid attention to what her parents told her and believed with all her heart they spoke wisdom and truth, such as when Harrison used a pet phrase, "It pays to be somebody," which to him meant it pays to have a good reputation, to do right, and be honest. He said it would come back and benefit you in some way. Her mother Alice told Bill that boys liked nice girls, making Bill want to be a nice girl so boys would like her. "I wouldn't have had sex with a boyfriend for anything," she said. She trusted her parents because they set good examples.

Although Alice never dwelled on her illnesses, she was unwell her entire life. Bill whispered in anger once that Doc had given Great Grandma Lizzie a sexually transmitted disease when she was pregnant with Alice, her thirteenth child. And, Alice had written in her journal, "I came into the world a sickly baby." At a few months old, she had boils on her and Doc lanced one that her mother told her left a place big enough to set a tea cup.

When Alice married Harrison at age sixteen, she began having spells of inflammatory rheumatism where she could not turn over in bed and had to be turned over in a sheet. She was unable to sleep or to get up and walk. Her doctor tried different kinds of medicine, but the pain always came back. After trying several of those remedies, Lizzie made a tonic out of different roots and herbs. It wasn't long until Alice got relief and then claimed she was cured, as she never had another spell of rheumatism. When she was twenty-six, she had what she called a "nervous breakdown." After getting her energy back and recovering from the nervous breakdown, she had another baby, developing a serious blood poisoning that made for a difficult and long recovery.

Alice was able to run a thriving household with Bill's help. When Alice would get pregnant, Bill was heartbroken because she knew the work load ahead for her and her twin sister, Evelyn, would increase. Jessie, their older brother, was no help at all, and Evelyn was good at getting out of the housework and finding other things to do. She was more of a reader than respectable help around the house. Plus, Evelyn didn't care for nice clothes or take care of what she had the way Bill did. They didn't have a closet in the upstairs bedroom they shared. For hanging clothes they had a wire strung from one corner to another. Evelyn threw her clothes over the wire while Bill starched and ironed her few things and hung them on hangers.

The house was cold in the winters, since they heated with wood and cooked on a woodstove, which only warmed the rooms they were in. The fires went out at night, and by morning the floors felt like ice on their feet. Bill once dampened her hair to wave and curl, and the waves froze on her head it was so cold. They warmed their cold plates before putting hot food on them; otherwise the food immediately turned cold.

Alice had her second set of twins the year Bill was a senior in high school. "I was killed," Bill said. She had to miss two weeks of school helping with the cooking, cleaning, and the care of the new babies, one a girl, Sammy Lane, and the other a boy, Kenneth Ronald.

Washing the laundry was done by heating water on a woodstove, or sometimes on a fire outside, placing it in a big tub, adding soap, and dumping in the dirty clothes. They stirred it around with a stick and then scrubbed each piece up and down on a gray, wavy tin rub board. From there the clothes were placed in a tub of clean rinse water, each piece wrung out by hand and pinned on a clothesline to dry. One day, with the washing done before lunch, they decided to go pick blackberries since they were ripe. They carried lard buckets two miles and picked until the buckets were full and carried them home to cook on the woodstove to can. They brought them to a boil and poured them in clean quart jars, adding forty quarts of blackberries to their stash of canned food. Without canning, they didn't have food for winter. Even if a grocery store had been close, money was in short supply.

Bill went back to Yellville High School that year, worrying about leaving her mother alone to care for the babies and run the home by herself. Every other Monday was laundry day, and she'd miss school to stay home and help Alice do the big wash. A girlfriend at school told her that on those days when the teacher would call roll and say, "Mary Willodean Smith," a class member would yell back, "She had to stay home and wash."

"Just killed me," Bill said, "but you know my roots go down deep. I learned to get tough and stay with something and do the hard things. When there's a drought, I could go through it. When there is no rain, I can rely on moisture down deep."

All the children in Bill's family went barefoot during the summer. Jessie was the oldest, then Bill and Evelyn, Bennie, Leroy, Billy Frank, Mary Elizabeth, and Sammy, and Ronald. They found all kinds of ways to entertain themselves. From watching chickens lay eggs to tying a piece of corn on a string, letting a chicken eat it, and then jerking it back out of the chicken's mouth. They made stilts and walked around on them. Bill's favorite thing was to find boards and use them like a sled on the steep side of a nearby holler.

A young man in the Mull community was "struck on me," Bill recalled, "and he drove a Model T car." She, Grandma Alice, Sammy, and Mary Elizabeth, nicknamed "Wig," were all sitting on the front porch drinking sweet tea in tall green glasses with clear pedestals, trying to fan away the heat of a hot summer afternoon. They were laughing and kidding Bill about the boy liking her. She mentioned she'd be embarrassed to go out with him because his car was so old. Jessie's friend said, "I wouldn't be as ashamed to do that as I would to go around barefooted like you do." Bill didn't have any shoes for casual, everyday wear. She saved the only good pair for school, church, and going to town. After Jessie's friend said that, Bill just went inside to a closet and sat there for hours, crushed with shame at someone not just noticing but pointing out she was so poor she didn't have shoes to wear.

Times were hard for Bill going to high school during the Depression, being the oldest girl of a family with nine children and a sickly mother. Although Harrison was a hard worker and intelligent, his work was not consistent. He taught school some of the months out of the year, raised and sold vegetables, farmed, and worked in the mines, but there was no steady income.

Bill never had a slip or a pair of socks all through high school. I suppose that's why she knew Pollyanna sayings like, "I worried because I had no shoes and then I saw a man who had no feet." She taught me a song when I would pout about not having new shoes for Easter, or some such piddly woe:

Nobody loves me
Everybody hates me
I could eat worms all daaaaaayyyyyy
First you bite the heads off
Then you suck the juice out
Then you throw the skins awaaaaayyy

By the time I finished singing the silly song, my sorrow was laughed away, far away. Even though she managed well, Bill never forgot what it was like to be poor. She always remembered the feel of the hole in the elbow of her coat when she was a senior in high school. It was a short coat that had been cut off an older long coat with holes in the elbows of both sleeves.

Clothing was hard to come by then, even though Grandma Alice was an excellent seamstress. She could look at a dress in a picture and cut out a pattern for it. She even made silk condoms for the women in her neighborhood. Of course, this is something that was not talked about. I don't know where she got her patterns for those. But even cheap print that sold for seven cents a yard had to be paid for, so without money it couldn't be bought. Bill said she pined away for a corduroy skirt when she was in school. Another student wore a man's white shirt with a corduroy skirt and Bill thought that was so stylish. She had an eye for smart design and knew how to be classy with what she could muster together.

Once in the winter of her senior year, the only clean thing she had to wear to school was a cotton summer dress with a low cut-out back. She decided to wear it and keep her coat on so she wouldn't freeze. That way no one would know that was all she had to wear. When she walked into her Home Economics class, she sat down with her coat on. The teacher called roll and noticed Bill was wearing her coat, and said, "Willodean, please take your coat off and hang it on the rack." Bill said she was mortified but walked to the coat rack, took off her coat, hung it up, and exposed her backless summer dress. Laughter from classmates filled the room.

Little has changed, other than the people, in the South Highway 14 community. The back roads are still unpaved, dusty and rocky; when it rains the tree limbs lean into green branch and wildflower tunnels that play over lanes with the sun lacing through. Black metal mailboxes along the roads here and there hint someone lives down a deserted-looking path. The little trails are lonesome and sing their stories of yesterday, of Davenports, Lynches, Manzer sisters left without parents, Shipmans, Dillards, Smiths, McClains, and more; stories of love, suffering, and wonder, a delicious array of awe at what must have been and what is gone forever except to God. The loneliness and the harshness of the land enrich its bloody raw breathless halt as if it were a time warp of nothingness other than quiet and divine stillness.

Chapter Four

AN EDUCATION
AND THE CCC

"YOU ARE LYING; I know you are lying through your teeth," I told my father. "That's the worst story I've ever heard. You just made that up."

"Am not lying. I'll swear on a stack of Bibles, it's the damn truth, the whole truth and nothing but the truth; am not lying." He playfully protested his story as he stretched back in his recliner and rubbed his hands on his knees.

Joe had said that when he was in the fourth grade his mother, Rena, packed his lunch in a small lard bucket with a tight lid. All she had to put in it that morning was cold pinto beans, a leftover piece of corn bread, and a few red radishes from the garden. She'd cut the corn bread in half and spread purple grape jelly inside. Usually, he and his brother, Jorden, tried to leave early but they'd had extra chores that morning and were running a little late getting out the door. Their classmates were already inside when they arrived at school. Joe walked up the side entry steps, opened the door and tripped over a step, and fell face forward. The bucket of beans hit the floor and exploded like a can of paint shooting brown and purple all over the floor, teacher's desk, and even hit a few kids sitting on the front row.

He said he could still hear the howls of laughter and feel the cloud of shame and embarrassment in his chest. "I'll never forget that," he said. "There was beans rolling around like marbles and clumps of purple all over, and them damn red radishes rolling around on the floor." And, since the door was at the side of the school house, and kids were already in their seats, it was like he was on a stage performing his "poor kid with beans for lunch act" for everyone.

Not long after that day, Joe quit school to help his mother and father on the farm. He was tired of being embarrassed from one thing after another, and not just being so poor he had to take beans for lunch. He'd miss days of school at times when a crop of corn had to be planted or cotton had to be harvested. The farming chores were more urgent than school. His parents couldn't manage well without his and his brothers' help during those critical times. And, then, because he would miss so much school work, when he went back, he wouldn't be able to catch up with the reading and homework assignments in order to pass tests. The teacher would be forced to hold him back a grade to catch up. He had flunked a couple grades and had to repeat them. But flunking didn't stop him from growing, and he was tall to begin with. When he'd go back to school the next year, he'd tower over the other little kids like some kind of superhero.

Added to the other reasons, he was embarrassed because of the clothes he had to wear. His mother couldn't afford to buy store-bought pants. She was a good seamstress and made all her boys' clothing. Yet, the only fabric she could afford to use was the burlap and gunny sack material that came with feed for the animals. When he decided to quit, in the fourth grade, neither Rena nor George encouraged him to go back. That was around the year 1932, when the Great Depression was in full force. They were worried about feeding five boys, and not about education, I'm sure.

Joe began to hear friends and neighbors talk about the Civilian Conservation Corps (CCC) when he was in his late teens. The news was that Roosevelt had started it to help young men get on the right track. Plus work was hard to find and many folks were tired and hopeless from the raw Depression years of struggle during the 1930s.

He was feeling restless, like he needed a change and needed to get out on his own. All he'd ever really done was work on a farm: milk cows, plant crops, build fence, care for hogs, chickens, mules, and horses, and help his mother with the vegetable garden: planting, hoeing, weeding, picking and canning vegetables and fruit.

Once Roosevelt was elected, he wasted no time calling the 73rd Congress into Emergency Session in 1933 to hear about and authorize the Civilian Conservation Corps program, which was part of the New Deal. The purpose of this program was to salvage our young men who could not find jobs in the private sector and train them to conserve the country's natural resources by planting trees, fighting forest fires, building dams for water supplies, building terraces to prevent soil erosion and building bridges over streams.

Roosevelt planned to fight against soil erosion and declining timber resources by utilizing unemployed young men from large urban areas. In the early 1930s a large number of young men roamed the cities and the countryside looking for work. More than twenty-five percent of the country's population was unemployed, hungry and without hope. Roosevelt feared that without training, a whole generation of young men would be without jobs and training, making them unprepared to assume financial responsibilities of home and family. Also, many of these young men suffered from lack of physical and spiritual nourishment.

Not everyone was eligible for the CCC. A man had to be between the ages of eighteen and twenty-five, unmarried, and a United States citizen. One condition of the enrollee was that $25.00 of the $30.00 a month pay would be sent home to assist their dependent family. The CCC had great public support from all political parties. It would not take long for the $25.00 allotment check to families at home to boost the economy across the nation. People at home would have life a little easier, finally. In communities close to the camps, local purchases averaged $5,000.00 a month in meeting the needs of the average two hundred CCC boys in a camp. Many small businesses would be kept alive by the CCC.

Joe was nineteen when he kissed Rena and George goodbye and walked to the town of Newark to catch his ride. As many poor young men did, he had raced to sign up for the work program as soon as he turned eighteen. The U.S. Army provided transportation for Joe and two other young men from Batesville to their appointed work site. They drove a few hours to South Highway 14 Buffalo River crossing, and then two more miles north before turning right onto a small dirt road that led to the CCC camp. Rows of bunk houses were lined up, and a table for processing the new recruits was set up where each man checked in by showing his birth certificate and answering all the family and physical health questions. Once that was completed, Joe was issued work clothes and told where his bunk would be. He was scheduled for a physical and dental exam, which would be his first ever, before he'd be given his work assignment.

Joe signed up to do general carpentry and drive a truck. I'm sure his lack of a high school education limited his job opportunities. Even though he could read and write and do some math, he was slow using those skills; however, he was smart enough to know there were many things he did not know, so he was cautious and timid about what he tried. He'd never traveled out of Arkansas and his reading had been limited due to his reading level and available reading material. He'd probably never read a children's book or a comic book. When he was older, he loved to read and kept a western beside his chair all the time. Maybe through the years he taught himself to read better by practicing.

What he did know for sure was how to work. He'd say, "About all I ever knew how to do was work!" And, he was quick to learn because he listened with his antenna ever on the lookout for information. He also valued people and talked to them and asked questions as if he were interviewing them with a microphone in his hand. He could spend an hour with someone and tell you that person's life story. "Where you from?" he'd ask. "What do you think about the news?" Usually it was the beginning of a long conversation and ones he remembered. If someone was just blowing and not a good source of information, he'd just throw what they said over his shoulder and move on. But, he was insightful of good information, too. He screened information about politics, current events, people, and wisdom. If he said it once, he said it a thousand times, "By God, a man has to crawl before he can walk," meaning few are successful without working hard first. He was able to put information in a context of history and time periods and categorize it into an education.

Joe had not been to many parties when he was nineteen, only a few church picnics now and then. He was innocent but standing by for adventure. After arriving at the CCC, he saw the other guys going to church, pie suppers, and local homes for singings. Soon he was in the middle of the activity. He was especially looking forward to Saturday night after catching glimpses of a girl he wanted to meet when he went to church the first Sunday he was in Mull. She had triggered something deep in him, even though she had rushed out with friends before he could meet her. Later he asked an acquaintance, Odale Davenport, a local who lived in his tent and bunked near him, if he knew the tall, thin girl with black hair. Odale said she was his cousin, and her name was Mary Willodean Smith, but most everyone called her "Bill." Her family lived in the little white house across from the Mull church on the way to Buffalo Park where all the CCC boys drove daily to work and back. He told Joe he'd introduce them the next time he got a chance.

A pie supper was being held Saturday night at the school house, which also served as a community center for local activities. Since Joe had been assigned a GMC truck for his job, he used it occasionally for other activities. Seven o'clock rolled around and he gathered up the other guys going to the local gathering and they headed south on Highway 14, turning on to Caney Road, a dusty, rough gravel road leading to the school building, directly across and down the road from the cobblestone Mull church. Joe was hoping Bill would be there and determined to meet her this time. Odale had promised.

Joe was a little nervous. People were inside standing around talking and drinking sweet tea and lemonade. Odale motioned to him from across the room. He saw Bill standing with a group of women. She was tall, about five feet eight, thin and curvy with shiny, long hair, and wearing a white blouse and a dark skirt with brown, worn loafers. Her laugh and warmth drew him toward her as he dug deeply for courage to meet her. Odale tapped her on the shoulder and said, "Bill, I want you to meet a friend from camp. This is Joe." Odale smiled, turned and left.

"Hello, I'm Bill."

"Joe Barnes is my name. I'm from down around Batesville. I've only been here a few weeks but I'm about to get settled in and catch the hang of how things work. I saw you last week at church, but didn't get to meet you."

"I stick pretty close to Mull so I'm not hard to find," she laughed. She told him she was one of the Smith twins. The other one's name was Evelyn, and she was dating Bill McClain from over around Maumee. She told him she had seven other brothers and sisters, and they lived in the little white house with the front porch, right off South Highway 14 across from the church. She asked him why he joined the CCC, and they ended up talking the rest of the evening. He met more of her friends, Doretha and Marie Dillard who lived across the holler from the Smiths. He met her oldest brother, Jessie, who wasted no time proving he was quite a character, telling one joke after another. Jessie was, no doubt, the life of the party. As the evening was winding down, Joe asked Bill if he could drive her home. Even though his truck was loaded with CCC guys, she didn't mind. When they stopped at her house, he opened the truck door for her and put his arm around her as they walked to her front porch. No light was on. She looked up at this tall man; he leaned way down and placed his hand on the back of her head, drew her to him and gently kissed her lips.

Bill thought she had died and gone to heaven, she later proclaimed. And Joe was hooked for sure as he'd never seen such beauty.

Joe appreciated every day with the CCC. He liked the structure and the three square meals a day. Before coming there, he'd always bathed in a round steel washtub, with water heated on the woodstove. The first time he went to the bath house and took a shower, "I thought that was the best thing that had ever happened to me." Also, he liked the routine of three good meals, and waking up early to doing calisthenics, just like the soldiers in an army camp and how they made their beds according to army regulations.

Every morning a parade of trucks hauling men and equipment headed south on Highway 14, turning left on Highway 268 leading to the park where the biggest part of their work was being done. The recreational area had just been designated Buffalo State Park when Joe started working there, and it was up to the CCC boys to develop the plan for it. They built the roads and planned all the rock design work for the retaining walls. They found the rocks in the quarry down by the Indian Rock House, and transported them to wherever they were needed. They built the log lodge high on the mountain that overlooks the river, and they built a pavilion and all six of the rustic cabins. Although the cabins appeared similar on the exterior, four different design plans were used. The rustic design, a hallmark of theirs, utilized native building materials of the local area to blend with and complement the natural environment. Every detail of the structures was considered important to the plan, whether it was a small rock path or the slope of the roof. Today the cabins are considered the most historically intact of the work done by the CCC in all of Arkansas. Vacationers have used them for more than sixty years. This park became part of the Buffalo National River system in 1972, the first designated national river in the nation.

When the CCC was in full swing and World War II loomed in the horizon, a national debate began as to whether these young men should have been prepared for military service and readiness or if they should have been used in the CCC. According to the "tone" of a newspaper article in the *Atlanta Constitution* in June of 1940 written by Harold Martin and reprinted in *Memories of Civilian Conservation Corps*, there was a group of people who felt the country had failed to help defend it by using the nation's young men in the camps instead of military services. Furthermore, the article went on to say how the boys of the CCC had learned things that made them vital in the system of national defense and they were too valuable to be handed a gun.

These young men knew how to tear down engines and build them back which is exactly what Joe Barnes would do later when he was with the Army in Iceland on the way to France later in WWII. Thousands of the CCC boys knew the workings of engines from using tractors on their farms. Martin stated, "Modern war travels on its machines and the CCC mechanic would fit perfectly into the personnel of a mechanized division." (page 6 of the *Memories of Civilian Conservation Corps*) He compared driving and caring for a tank as similar to driving and caring for a tractor. Many of them were welders, telephone men, expert woodworkers who could as easily make a truck cab as a wood frame they'd made for other things such as wooden pontoons for bridges. Some were surveyors, field radio operators, parachute experts who had trained in fighting fires in backwoods areas where no tractor could go. Some were photographers who learned to do mapping. They all knew first aid. They built their own barracks which were no different than ones they might build in war. Some were expert carpenters. There were cooks who followed the same standards as military cooks with the same utensils, the same order of cleanliness, quality and table manners.

In one sense these men were already soldiers when they were later drafted into the service. They rose at 5:30 a.m. to a whistle instead of a bugle. They wore fatigues. They went to breakfast at 6 o'clock and did calisthenics every morning. They policed the area. They made their beds with the same regulation fold-back as the cadets at West Point did. They stood for roll call. They even used Army terminology such as a "company" of men and a "crew" squad. A leader might be an "assistant" instead of a corporal. The CCC men became "specialists" who would later utilize skills in war as the WWII loomed around the corner. They would have the expertise to keep motors and wheels turning, keep communication flowing between units by telephone and radio, repair broken tanks, rebuild bridges, and perform a thousand duties needed in the military.

For the most part, the CCC boys knew nothing of such a debate. They were simply doing their job every day and concerned about the draft. Joe and Bill kept dating when they could steal the time. She'd had many boyfriends before Joe, who had had few girlfriends. She'd almost said "yes" to a proposal by a local young man, Charlie Hill, but when he said he wanted to live the rest of his life on South 14, she declined. "That turned my stomach," she said. Joe made a good impression wherever he went. He was tall and handsome and carried himself with humility and a casual, natural poise. He was a manly man and knew his place; he was not loud or a braggart. He had a quiet presence that drew people and invited them toward him. And, Bill had some of the same qualities. She was a beauty, poised and elegant. Loved by all she met. Harrison, her father always said of her: "Bill, she is the stake of life," meaning his daughter was strong and wise; she had what it took!

Neither Bill nor Joe carried an extra ounce of fat as food choices, unlike today, were limited. Bill was colorful. She loved to dance and could jig with the best of folks. When the guitar or piano started playing, she'd begin to tap and pound her feet to the music and close her eyes and hold her head up with her elbows bent, snapping her fingers in time. She'd lose herself, and didn't care what she looked like when she was dancing. She played both the piano and the guitar. She was twenty years old when she met Joe.

After their first date, Joe came to Bill's house every chance he had. They went to local activities on the weekends, went to church, and went to the Buffalo to swim. Sometimes they just parked, and did what Bill called "sparking."

While they were dating, Jessie, Bill's oldest brother, used to hear the CCC trucks coming down the dirt road and he would gather the Smith children and have one positioned in each of the side windows of the house and the two windows in the front. He'd have them yell and scream and wave and bang on the side of the house as the CCC trucks drove by. The more noise they made, the more he rewarded the kids. Jessie was trying to make his sister mad and he was trying to make it look like that Smith bunch was crazy to scare Joe away from dating Bill. "But nothing could have scared Joe away from me, I don't reckon," she always said with a romantic drawl.

Getting to know the Smith family was poles apart from his family. Much more lighthearted, the Smiths teased each other and joked around. All the boys (Jessie, Bennie, Billy Frank, Leroy, and Ronald) and the girls (Evelyn, Sammy Lane, and Mary Elizabeth, nicknamed "Wig") were outgoing. When Bill was younger, Jessie told her the proper way to eat beans was to line them up on her knife. After that, she lined up her beans on a knife, even though she was the only one at the table that used that skill. She wanted to be proper, until finally it hit her that Jessie had tricked her again. He had tricked her many times. Once he gave her a Bible verse for her to memorize and say out loud in church when it was her turn. Every Sunday at the Mull Church of Christ, after singing the first hymn, the children were asked to recite a memory verse. When it was Bill's turn, she said, "Moses wept, Paul crept, and Jesus took it afoot." Smirks and giggles and hand over mouth laughter waved through the pews. Bill was younger than Jessie and she said for years she believed everything he said, but at times she thought she might be a little nuts because of the way she trusted Jessie and didn't question him, just did whatever he told her.

Joe's family was more serious, burdened with life, health issues, working, saving and having enough to eat. At first, the Smiths' fun-loving way of life felt foreign to him, but he didn't run. He stood back and observed how they related. He liked having fun and enjoyed the casual, playful affection between them all. Bill began to open up to him and tell him how hard their lives had been during the Depression, the same as his. Her parents, Harrison and Alice, had moved to Mull in 1919 when she and her twin, Evelyn, were ten months old. Harrison had worked as a foreman in the Sure Pop zinc mine north of Maumee above Water Creek. Wagon travel was rough, which isolated both of them from their families. The isolation and hardship became more than either of them wanted or could bear. The little house they had moved into at Mull wasn't much more than a shack. Alice always said, "We were poor, but we had lots of love." Bill told Joe her most difficult time came in 1936, the year she was a senior in high school. Alice was pregnant for the seventh time and Bill was devastated when her senior year was interrupted by having to help her mother.

Joe liked Bill's honesty and openness. Her family talked about even the sad and painful sides of life whereas his family members were more closed and secretive about those things. Joe was different than other guys Bill had dated. He seemed to have a strong presence, even though humble and never expected much. Instead he was grateful for anything. She saw he was honest and wanted to do what was right. He told her about his mother, Rena, and how she'd been given to a farm family named J.M. and Martha Finch when she was two months old. They'd lived in a small place called Big Bottoms close to Newark, Arkansas. Rena's mother, Anna Bowers, apparently had a "nervous breakdown" after her husband deserted her, leaving her with two older children and an infant. The last heard of her was that she had gone to the Booneville Sanatorium in Booneville, Arkansas. Joe spoke of his mother with sadness and gentleness. He had wanted to please her and make her proud of him.

Bill loved Joe's warmth and compassion toward his mother. She felt the same way for her own mother and listened and followed all her advice. Harrison's saying, "It pays to be somebody," seemed to describe Joe.

War news was heating up and the CCC boys knew before long they would be drafted or join the Army. Joe had stretched his skills as a carpenter working on the cabins in the park. He laid some rock on the retaining walls, and transported men and supplies in the GMC truck assigned to him. He knew he was about to be drafted, but instead of waiting on that, he went with some of his friends and joined the U.S. Army. He returned to Mull and, even though they had dated only three months, asked Bill if she would marry him before he left. He didn't want to risk her not being there when he returned.

"When he asked me to marry him, I hugged him and didn't want to ever let go, but honestly all I could think about was that I didn't have a dress to wear!" Bill said. "When I told Joe, he said he'd go to town and buy me one. I thought wow, now there's the man I want to marry." The next day he walked twenty-eight miles to Marshall to buy her a dress. He picked out one that was a soft rose color made out of silk crepe. It cost $3.00 and fit Bill like a glove.

The following day they walked to Buffalo Park in their dress clothes and found a Justice of the Peace named Mr. White, who Joe knew was working on the road. He stopped working and they all stood in the middle of a curve on the road which threaded through the tall green pines and oaks ending at the Buffalo. Tree limbs from each side of the road stretched to touch making a green shadowed arch for them to pause and say their vows. No music but the wind whistling through the trees.

Joe and Bill walked back to the Smith home and cel-ebrated with everyone they could find, and then honeymooned in the back bedroom. Alice had cleaned the back room for them, but Bill said, "It wouldn't have mattered if it had been dirty; we wouldn't have noticed if you know what I mean." There wasn't a door or even a curtain over the open space. It was April 7, 1941.

On June 14, 1941, Joe was inducted into the U.S. Army.

Chapter Five

PIONEERS ALONG
THE BUFFALO

ACK ROADS ARE LIKE bumpy washboards, with hard packed, dusty dirt and limestone rocks. Hills fall off into steep hollers and treacherous ravines. Buffalo gnats swarm in little clouds, attacking the eyes and ears. Ticks hide on weeds, limbs, and leaves, lurking to land and ready to bite and attach to soft warm skin. Chiggers, tiny, almost invisible red bugs, beg you to claw at your skin until it bleeds. Copperheads and rattlesnakes lie coiled and waiting beneath rocks and foliage. After spring rains pound for days and the river and creeks flood, summer temperatures turn to stifling ninety and one hundred degrees for days and weeks. Then, the blessed creeks and rivers get low and by late August some dry up. It's a hard land.

My mother was born in one of the roughest, most isolated places imaginable, Sure Pop, Arkansas, in Marion County in 1918. It was not a happy time for her mother, my Grandmother Alice, one of fourteen children—ten boys and four girls. Since marrying Harrison Smith when she turned sixteen, they'd moved to the tiny mining community close to Maumee, up the creek from Maude's Hole, the coldest, clearest swimming hole around.

The closest town of any size was Yellville, fourteen miles north. No roads existed, so people followed the creeks or animal trails and paths. From Maumee, one of the first Arkansas mining towns, they traveled by horseback, by wagon or by foot up Water Creek to another creek called Camp Creek and on to Yellville from there. The lead and zinc mines at Maumee, the second largest ore company in the United States, were in use from 1912 to the early 1920s, employing more than one hundred men in the big mine and mill. Ore was loaded on wagons and hauled to Gilbert, twelve miles west up the river. Bill McClain, who grew up there, said, "Sometime you would see a string of wagons a mile long; they looked like a wagon train." Other than working in the mines, people made a living by farming cotton, corn, and hay on the ridges surrounding Maumee.

During the mining boom, Maumee boasted a large general merchandise store, a post office, a twenty-seven-room hotel, four general stores, a blacksmith shop, a barber shop and at least thirty residential homes. More than 150 kids from the nearby hills and hollers attended school there. Some lived so far they'd have to start walking before daylight, carry a lantern to light their way, hide it at daylight, and then pick it up on the way home.

Alice's parents, Doc (James Franklin Dillard) and Lizzie (Nancy Elizabeth Smith Dillard), moved to Arkansas after getting married in Bamy County, Missouri in September, 1881. She said when they moved to Clabber Creek, northeast of Rush Creek where she was born, there wasn't a house or any cleared land. It was all wooded, rough hills. Doc built the house and cleared the land by himself. He split the rails to fence his property and made a corn crop for his family to use and to sell. She said he worked more than eight hours a day, seven days a week, "and no coffee breaks." While living there, Doc would take a wagon to Springfield, Missouri, and haul food and necessities back to the area and sell them to merchants in Marion County. He would be gone for weeks at a time. Bill recalled her Grandmother Lizzie saying she got so lonely at times, "I would have been glad to seen a dog coming down the road."

Doc became quite a businessman for someone with no education. He built caskets and sold them. He built a sawmill where his sons worked with him. The *Mountain Echo* once wrote in the *Rush* news, "Doc Dillard last week sawed and dressed 3,200 feet of lumber in 4 hours and during that time ground 23 bushels of corn." If someone moved to the community and needed a place to live, Doc would oversee the building of a home for them and have the newcomers a house built in a few days. He acquired the name Doc because he had to be the "doctor" for his family with home remedies. Mom remembered him making tooth pullers in his blacksmith shop once when his son Clarence had a terrible toothache and they were unable to get him to a dentist.

Sick or dying people didn't go to the hospital. Instead, neighbors sat up all night with the person, and when someone passed away, it was always in their home. Neighbors and women would wash the body, and lay it out covered with a white sheet, until they got the shroud made. When Doc made a coffin from his own lumber, he would cover the outside with black satin and the inside with white muslin, and place lace around the top. He didn't charge a family for the coffin if they couldn't afford it.

With fourteen children, one can only imagine the cooking, cleaning, washings and managing the home that Lizzie did. The children's' names: Guy, Arthur, Roy, Ira, Pate, Clarence, Bazze, Ted, Frank, Rosa, Mabel, Alice, Oscar, and another little boy never named.

Doc and Lizzie were well known for the plentiful food they had the year around. They'd spread out a feast when it came time for a holiday meal. Alice wrote in her journal:

> *The food didn't come from the super market. There would be turkey and dressing or big fat hens with dressing, home cured ham boiled or baked, several kinds of cakes and pies, sausage, boiled back bones, all kinds of jellies and jams, preserves, hominy, molasses, different—all kinds of vegetables, and canned fruit. I just wonder what a dinner like that would cost now. Dear reader I am not exaggerating. My dad could have more to eat around our place than any place I've ever seen, not only was our smoke house filled with pork, he usually killed a beef every fall when it got cold. He'd*

dress it and hang it up. We could have steak or roast any time along with boiled beef and sweet potatoes. I don't know just how my mother cooked them together some way, and it surely was delicious, and sometimes we could have a deer or two hanging in the smoke house and when the snow was falling no one had to worry about going hungry. There was always lots of fire wood and two big fire places. We didn't get cold either. Times surely are different now.

Lizzie made her own lye using an ash hopper. She would empty ashes from their fireplace and when it rained on them, the water ran through the ashes and it would come out lye for soap making. She thought it was terribly extravagant and wasteful to buy soap.

Even though Doc was a good provider and a leader in the community, he had a dark side. It was told that he was a hard drinker and a womanizer. Bill said when she was in her teens, she and Evelyn were playing in the barn and, "He [Doc] tried to mess with me." She ran back in the house and told her mother who said, "Don't go back around him alone, ever, and don't tell your daddy, because he'd kill him." Other family members have whispered of these things but most have remained silent. Of course, Lizzie knew all these things about her husband, and must have become overwhelmed at times with running a household for so many people, under such hard conditions. She was seen walking off into the woods alone where she'd be gone for hours and then return and start all over with the work and the weight of the harsh pioneer lifestyle and the hard land. Their home was the first built in the Mull community, which was initially called Dillard, and later changed to Mull.

Not much is known about Doc's family history. Nothing is known of his father, and indications show that maybe his mother was never married. Doc could not read or write. Once when someone wrote a letter for him and had trouble spelling a word, the writer asked someone nearby, "How do you spell this man's name?" Doc told him, "Don't spell it; just put it down."

As Mull began to grow with additional school-age children walking miles to Rush and other schools, Doc Dillard decided to organize and build a school so they wouldn't have to travel such a long, hard distance. He called a meeting and had directors elected, and they got together and built a schoolhouse down the Caney Road across from the Mull church. Benjamin Harrison Smith was hired as the first school teacher. He was the local intellectual as he read everything he could get his hands on: newspapers, books, magazines. At that time, a test was given to prospective teachers to determine what they knew. They were given a certificate to teach up to the grade level of their education.

He boarded with Doc and Lizzie, who lived nearby in a house called a "dog trot," named for the way it could be used by dogs to simply trot through the middle. A twelve-foot hall cut down between the living areas helped to suck the wind through making it breezy and cool. All the bedrooms were on one side because they didn't heat where they slept. They only heated the other side which was the kitchen and the living room.

The first school session, at $25.00 per month, lasted only two months because that's all they could afford to pay. Alice, one of Harrison's students, got caught passing a note one time and stuffed it in her bra to keep Harrison from getting it, since it was about the girls talking about him. Alice had learned to outsmart about anyone since she'd grown up being teased and tormented by ten brothers.

Harrison and Alice fell in love and started dating when she was fifteen, and it wasn't long until he proposed. Doc and Lizzie gave their blessing when she turned sixteen. Harrison was twenty-five. Teaching school wasn't enough income to start a young family and the two decided to move close to Maumee where Harrison got a job as a foreman in one of the Sure Pop mines.

As with the Dillard family, the hardness of the land hadn't stopped Harrison's parents from settling in the area. John Smith and Julia Ann Burns came from North Carolina through the Cumberland Gap into Kentucky and Tennessee, first discovered in 1776 by Daniel Boone and Dr. Thomas Walker. Others followed them, starting with a group of settlers in covered wagons who traveled to Marion County by way of trails and pathways through southern Missouri. John and Julia most likely followed the route many did, through Taney County, Missouri, and turned south to Marion County where they settled near Water Creek in a place called Tomahawk Creek in Searcy County.

Their first child, William Thomas Marion Smith, was born in March 1858, and later married a sixteen year old, Miss Mary Missouri Carolina Moody who got her name from a pioneer custom to honor and keep records where she was born. Since her parents, the father a Baptist minister, were traveling through those states, they gave her both names. After settling in the area, Thomas and Mary had three young children: Wyley, John William, and a baby girl, Ann. Early one morning, Mary needed to walk to the creek for water. She remembered to move a gun, which hadn't been fired in a long time but was in sight on a high shelf in a cabinet. She pushed it back out of sight on the very top of the cabinet so it couldn't be reached or seen. As soon as she left, John William, who was three years old, climbed on the cabinet, got the gun and, while playing with it, accidentally shot himself. Mary heard a gunshot and, terrified, ran back to the house to find her son shot in the stomach. She grabbed him, and, holding him to her chest, ran two miles to the neighbors for help, but too late. Her other baby girl, Ann, died of typhoid a few days later. Both children were buried in the same casket.

Before Thomas and Mary settled in Freck, a tiny community between Maumee and Yellville, they made three trips to Indian Territory and one to Ft. Smith in a covered wagon to be ready for the land rush. An old *Mountain Echo* article, April 19, 1989, says the Smiths didn't like the harsh living conditions in Ft. Smith so they returned to Water Creek. Since Water Creek is such hard, rocky, hilly and remote land, Ft. Smith must have been like a nightmare out of the dark ages. Later, Thomas and Mary settled in their new home at

Freck, having nine more children, one of which was my grandfather, Benjamin Harrison.

The Buffalo River has been central to many little places like Freck since the Indians were pushed westward in the early 1800s. Until then few white men had seen the Buffalo. The Indians didn't keep records. The first white men, like the Dillards and the Smiths, were hunters and squatters and settlers who came in and took choice land for $1.25 an acre. Like pioneers in other areas, they lived with an abundance of wildlife, such as herds of buffalo, deer, and elk, for years. The wildlife and forests of hardwoods must have seemed endless to the first settlers.

Around 1905, about 27,000 people lived in the Buffalo's 1338 square mile watershed. By 1965 outmigration had reduced the area's population by more than half. Most of the country had limited resources of wildlife and a forest of slow-growing hardwoods on rocky soils, which were largely gone within a century.

The river flows through Newton, Searcy, Marion, and Baxter Counties in Northwest Arkansas from west to east. It originates in the highest part of the Boston Mountains in the Ozarks, flows out onto the Springfield Plateau near the historic community of Erbie and then crosses the Salem Plateau before it joins the White River. The most challenging section of the river to float is the fifteen mile section upriver from Boxley. Advanced canoeists call it the Hailstone River. But depending on who you talk to, some don't even measure that as part of the main river. Those that do, measure the river at 153 miles long. Without it, starting at Ponca, to the White River is 125 miles.

After Alice and Harrison moved to Sure Pop, she kept house, cooked and cared for her first child, a boy, Jessie, while Harrison worked in the mines. Once she married, she simply did what she'd always seen her mother do. And, she'd heard her mother talk about how lonesome she'd been when she was a newlywed at Clabber Creek, before the town of Rush became a booming mining town. No one else lived near them. Doc had found and cleared the land himself, built the house and split rails to fence his land. He would take a wagon to Springfield, Missouri, and haul food and necessities back and sell to merchants in Marion County. He kept some for the family's personal stock. Alice rarely saw anyone besides Harrison and Jessie in Sure Pop. When she got pregnant with their second child, she knew a move wasn't likely.

They'd planned when her due date came close, she and Harrison would take the wagon to her mother's near Mull. They would call the doctor from Yellville and that way Alice would have help with Jessie, and a doctor for delivering the baby.

But that plan unraveled when Jessie got sick and developed a high fever, followed by Harrison coming down with the same illness. Traveling was out until both got better. Alice was nine months pregnant by then, in the dead of winter, and caring for Jessie and Harrison. Late one evening, when it began to snow, she carried in as much wood as she could with her large belly, knowing they'd be in a pickle without firewood. Harrison's fever became high and he literally could not move off the couch. Snow fell all night, reaching the top of the porch by next morning. Alice was worried but didn't panic. She waddled through the snow again that day to gather more wood. Four feet of snow had fallen to measure the biggest snow in Marion County history. She managed to cook enough to get by and feed everyone. That afternoon she saw someone riding a horse up their hill. Harrison's brother, Saren, despite the record-setting cold and snow, came to check on her, knowing her time to have the baby was close. After he saw she was okay and helped her carry in enough wood for a few days, he went home. The next day her father–in-law, Thomas, came to help. She fixed ham and gravy that evening and the weather was so cold she had to heat the plates so the gravy wouldn't get hard and too cold to eat.

That evening her labor pains began, and as they grew closer, Thomas stayed eventually riding a horse down the frozen creek to find the local midwife, Aunt Mary Williams. Fortunately, she knew Alice must have help, no matter what the weather was like. The midwife knew how to travel in the rugged Ozark Mountains. Since Water Creek was frozen and it was the short-est distance between her home and Alice's, she rode her horse straight up the creek to save time. Alice was grateful and relieved to see her that day. Even then, in that day and time, she couldn't imagine having a baby without a doctor or her mother, especially with

Harrison down so sick and a two-year-old, and no one to help. She felt like she was at the North Pole. When Mary walked in the door, she knew they could manage together. Then, it wasn't long until the baby came. Mary became confused as Alice began to have more labor pains. "My pains got worse again, instead of easing up, lo and behold, another baby came." Twins, two girls, and the first one she called Mary Willodean and the second, Evelyn, each weighing seven pounds. Aunt Mary Williams had never delivered twins before.

Alice said, "Aunt Mary knew I'd have to have her and she was such a good, kind soul, she came to help me in that weather without a moment's hesitation." That's why Mary became a legend in the Ozark hills. When interviewed at age seventy-seven, she said, "It's near seven hundred babies I've caught." She delivered babies in the hills of Searcy and Marion counties for years. She kept an accurate account until she got to six hundred. Her fee was $3.00 but rarely collected the full amount; instead she often collected some form of produce or goods instead of money. And there were times when the poor people had no way of paying her for the long night or the hard travel. Often, she'd have to walk the distance to the mother's home no matter what the weather or the condition of the river and creeks. She knew how to wade Water Creek or the Buffalo River. She knew the paths up steep, rocky hillsides and along rough ridges above the streams. Many times the mother needed her quickly, so Mary would have to hurry and take shortcuts. If the farm horses weren't needed in the fields, she would ride one to her patient's home. But, the needs of the farm came first. She lost only one mother—her own daughter-in-law—during all of her years of service as a midwife to the people of the Ozarks. She died in childbirth of "albuminuria." Alice said, "If things hadn't gone well for us that day I had twins, it would just have been too bad because travel was impossible for a doctor."

Not long after the twins were born, Alice wanted out of Sure Pop more than ever. When they were ten months old, the dreaded flu epidemic hit Arkansas. She and Harrison had gone to Freck to visit his family for the weekend when Harrison was hit with it. Thirty minutes after he started chilling, he became unconscious. Plus, he got double pneumonia and they all thought he would die. All his family visited him. Then, he gradually started getting better and they went home. Thomas came to check on his son and the young family. Harrison was still not well, and it wasn't long until Alice got the flu, too. Thomas took over and cared for Jessie and the baby girls. He had to milk the cow and wash the diapers, which he wasn't skillful at doing. Instead of rinsing the baby poop out of the diapers, he just built a fire, and got the water rolling, added the soap and dumped in the diapers, poop and all. Alice was appalled but too sick to make a scene, and instead turned her head and accepted it. "It didn't kill us," she said.

Bill loved her Grandfather Thomas's wife, her Grandmother Mary, who was half Cherokee and when she died at sixty, didn't have one gray hair. The harsh living may have taken its toll on Mary, unlike Thomas, who lived to be eighty-three.

After the flu epidemic, Alice again told Harrison, "I want out of Sure Pop." She prayed God would move her from the isolation there on Water Creek with no neighbors or family and travel all but impossible. She missed terribly all the activity of a big family at her parents' home. She said it wasn't too long until she thought she felt a hand on her shoulder and sensed the words, "I'll do something." Afterwards, Harrison came home from the mine one day and said, "We're moving; let's pack."

Alice recited old songs and ballads that had been passed down to her. She knew them by heart. It's no wonder they all were full of sadness and heartbreak:

The Drinking House Over the Way

The Room was so cold, so cheerless and bare,
Its rickety table and one broken chair,
Its curtainless window and hardly a pane,
To keep out the snow, the wind and the rain.
There all alone a pale woman was lying,
You need not look twice to see she was dying,
Dying of want and hunger and cold,
And this is the story, the story she told:

No, Momma I am no better,
My cough is so bad,
It's wearing me out, tho', and that makes me glad,
For it's wearisome living when one's all alone,
Yes Momma, I've a husband, He is somewhat about,

I hope he comes in before the fire goes out;
But I guess he is gone where he is likely to stay,
Gone to that drinking house over the way.

It's not always so and I hope you won't think
Too hard of him, lady.—it's only the drink.
You see it took sudden and grew very bad,
We had no doctor, the poor little lad.
His father was gone, never meaning to stay,
Gone to that drinking house over the way.

And when he came back, it was far in the night,
I was so tired, so sick with fright of
Staying so long with my baby alone,
And it cutting my heart with its pitiful moan.
No, momma, he was sober—at least mostly,
I think, for he always stayed away until he worked off
the drink,
But he swore at the child as panting he lay,
And went back to that drinking house over the way.

I heard the gate slam; my heart
Seemed to freeze like ice in my bosom,
And there on my knee by the side
Of the cradle all shivering I stayed,
I wanted my mother, I cried and I prayed.
My clock had struck 12, my baby was still;
My thoughts went back to my home on the hill,
Where my happy girlhood had spent her short days,
Far from that drinking house over the way.

Could I be that girl, I, the heartbroken wife,
While watching alone that dear little
Life was going so fast.
I had to bend low to see if –
His breath was so fast and so slow.
Yes, Momma, it was easy, his dying,
He just grew more white.
And his father came in just at break of day,
Came in from that drinking house over the way.

Our neighbors were kind; the minister came.
He talked to me, seeing our baby again,
Of the bright angels I wonder, if they
Can see in that drinking house over the way.

There is a verse in the Bible, the
Minister said. No drunkard can enter
The Kingdom, he said—and he is
My husband and I love him so,
And where I am going, I want him to go.

The baby and I both will want him there.
Don't you think the dear Savior will answer my
prayer?
And please, when I am gone ask someone to pray,
For him at that drinking house over the way.

There was no Highway 14 at Mull when Alice and Harrison moved their family from Sure Pop, only a trail, and travel by horse and wagon. And people were still following creeks to town. In 1919 a movement started to build a road from Yellville to Marshall crossing the Buffalo. Some wanted the road to cross the river at Maumee; others wanted the crossing just south of Mull. Doc Dillard, admired and respected by many people in the community, led the campaign for the road to cross close to Mull.

As the community grew, most of the back roads developed leading to the Buffalo River as it brought life to the area through fishing, hunting, transportation, and recreation. From where the cobblestone Church of Christ now sits, the dusty dirt roads twist around like a spider web somehow ending at the river. South of the church about half a mile the road starts to curve and go down where Highway 14 crosses the Buffalo and leads to the towns of Big Flat, Harriet, Marshall and on to Little Rock. From the church west the road winds to Caney Creek, Water Creek, and Maumee and down to the river or the town of Gilbert. Going north from the church and the first big dirt road east leads to the old town of Rush and the Rush landing on the Buffalo. Going south from the church before going down the river hill, the road curves left into Highway 268, dead ending at the main park. This intersection is where Joe and Bill bought 40 acres from her brother, Bennie for $400.00 after he returned from the war in 1945. They built their home in the fork of the intersection in 1948.

Chapter Six
___

JOE'S STORY IN WWII

$\mathcal{T}$HE CIVILIAN CONSERVATION CORPS boys
would not escape World War II. Many
joined before they were drafted as Joe did.
Bill said some local boys who didn't want to go acted
like they were crazy when interviewed so they would
get a mental health deferment. One was her cousin,
who would raise his arms up high and reach and grab
for things in the air no one else could see, as if he were
seeing bugs, making it look like he was psychotic.
And, it worked. He stayed home unlike so many of the
young but brave. Acting silly, family members would
mimic how he must have pretended, grabbing and
clawing at invisible bugs in the air.

Harrison, being the local news hound, kept everyone informed of current war activity. By 1940 war had
engulfed Europe and much of Asia. The United States
was preparing to put its military house in order. Many
Americans believed it was just a matter of time until
the country was drawn into a global conflict. According to all the news, America's leaders were working
to increase the size of the armed forces, and acquiring
modern equipment to strengthen our fighting force.

The CCC turned out to be like a prep school for the armed forces.

Joe and Bill were married two months when he had to leave for basic training. From the time they first met, they both knew the war was coming, making their future together unpredictable. Then, to further complicate their situation, Bill realized she was pregnant right before Joe had to go away.

Joe's first day of active duty was June 4th, 1941, at Fort Leonard Wood, Missouri, often called the "Fort Lost in the Woods," a few hours north of Marion County, Arkansas. After finishing his basic training, he participated in maneuvers in Arkansas and Louisiana, at which time he'd probably been assigned to the Fifth Infantry Division since they were training at those locations. Before leaving the States and going to Iceland for more training, his first child was born, a daughter, Shirley Jo. He was able to go home on furlough one time to see her before he left the country.

Joe's group left the States on seventy small shallow ships he called ferries. After ten days at sea all the ships but five went a different direction. Joe didn't know why or where the others went. He was in the smaller group of five and said about the time the ships split, torpedoes started firing everywhere. He thought they were looking for a German submarine. After seventeen days at sea, they arrived at Iceland in the spring of 1941. While there, they unloaded boats, built roads and buildings and maintained training schedules. Joe said he worked on putting trucks together from individual parts, such as windshields, motors, chassis, and wheels which were shipped separately. Then, the soldiers put them together as complete vehicles and shipped them to France.

He described Iceland as about as cold as it gets, sixty degrees below. The wind blew so hard he had to hold on to a rope to get to the mess hall. He wrote home and asked Bill to send him some hard candy he kept craving. The next day he went to the mess hall and bowls of hard candy were on all the tables, which was a pleasant memory, unlike Thanksgiving there. He had looked forward to a good Thanksgiving meal as the holiday approached. Turkey was one of his favorite foods. When the day arrived and lunchtime came, all the men waited impatiently in line more than excited for a big Thanksgiving meal. Joe's turn came, and he handed his tray to the cook serving food, who threw the bony end of the turkey wing on Joe's tray. "Damn," he said, "give me another piece of turkey; ain't no meat on that bone." The cook just shook his head...no. "I was never so sick in my life," Joe said.

For entertainment, the soldiers would go downtown Reykjavik and just shop and look around. Joe said there was a fish on every doorstep delivered by a local fisherman. When he first walked by the pastry shops, he was amazed at how beautiful and delicious the donuts and sweet rolls looked. Not being able to pass those up, Joe went in and bought a sack full, took them outside, and when he bit into one, "It tasted just like a fish," he said.

Outposting and defense of the Keflavik area in Iceland kept the troops busy for fifteen months. Most of the training activity was drudgery. In addition to putting trucks together, they did dock work, sodded huts, and fought the constant winds on long marches—all mixed in with submarine scares, plane crashes, and strafing attacks by German reconnaissance planes. Training became more interesting and active when they moved to England in August of 1943.

At Tidworth Barracks in England training was intensely directed toward the upcoming invasion of France. And, for the first time, restrictions were relaxed and passes and furloughs were issued freely, which never happened for the men of the Fifth while training in Iceland for well over a year.

In a few months, the Fifth Division moved to Camp Bullykinler and Camp Donard Ledge in the wet, stark hills of Northern Ireland for advanced training in preparation for the invasion of France. Rigorous combat training followed for eight months. Courses on battles, field problems, battle indoctrination, weapons courses, and refresher courses on all types of arms, gas schools, and amphibious land operations were included.

Joe said they trained in cleaning out buildings, loading and unloading on big trucks and loading and unloading on ships. In Newcastle, Ireland, they loaded on big trucks and drove to Belfast, then loaded on a ship and went back to Newcastle. A month later Joe, with three entire infantry divisions and a quartermaster, boarded a ship in Belfast.

On the eve of the departure for Normandy, generals Eisenhower and Patton flew in to Northern Ireland to inspect. Joe remembered every detail of that afternoon. They built a place, like a stage, for Patton to stand while the men sat in rows in front of him with their individual units. Patton flew in on a little plane that landed on a mesh strip which had been rolled out, providing a practical place to land. "He was the roughest looking man I ever saw," Joe said. He could quote Patton's speech verbatim:

> Men of the Fifth Division, we're going to France. I've come here to tell you I've chosen you to go to Berlin. And we're not going to crawl over there. [Joe would sit up in his recliner when he spoke this part and growl the words] If we crawl over there, the Germans will stick a pitchfork in your ass... If you'll remember, them damn Limmies came over and tried to take the U.S. and our old farmers just pulled off the plow handles and beat the sons of bitches back to sea...

Patton later remarked about these men, "This is the fittest, roughest, readiest outfit I have ever inspected." Finally, the Fifth was pronounced ready. The red diamond was the insignia of the Fifth Division and became a deep-rooted tradition that stands for intense loyalty and versatile performance with the motto, "We Will."

Bill followed Joe's whereabouts as much as possible without much access to news other than a radio, since phones and televisions were not yet fixtures in American homes. They had a radio, such as it was. Its reliability depended on the quality of the battery. And, they had the postal service. Even when Joe wrote her letters and she received them, he couldn't tell her where he was. Popa Harrison listened to radio news, and read every newspaper and news magazine he could find. In the evenings, the whole Smith clan gathered around the radio listening to Harrison's favorite journalist, Gabriel Heater. When radio reception was unbearable, a family member would run across the holler to the home of Pate and Cora, Alice's brother and sister-in-law. They always had a better battery and radio and Pate would know the very latest that had happened or was about to happen. When the battery wound down on the Smith radio, they'd pour water on it, giving it a boost to work a few more hours, at least until they could catch a ride to town or send for someone to buy a new one.

Mail was tightly censored both ways, so no details were mentioned about places or plans of battles. But, of course, everyone along with Bill knew about the Invasion of Normandy, and the days that followed. Each day she feared a telegram or a man in uniform might arrive at the house telling her Joe had been killed. Wives, children, parents, all Americans waited in agony by the radio for news of their loved ones.

A week before Joe's division landed on Utah Sugar Red Beach in the Sainte-Mere-Eglise area, an advance detachment had been sent to become acquainted with the situation and prepare for the division's landing. Near midnight on July 4, 1944, Joe's unit, Company B of the 11th Infantry Regiment, 5th Infantry Division, boarded the transport ship *Excelsior* for the voyage to

France. Five days later, after three years and twenty-five days of preparation and training, Joe finally landed at Utah Beach on July 9, 1944. From the coast of France to the Normandy beachhead, which had been won thirty-three days earlier, the 11th Infantry Regiment noisily climbed over the sides of the ships, down the swinging nets, and into the tossing landing crafts that would take them to Utah Sugar Red Beach. They had been in dress rehearsals, but this was the real thing. This was it. The Red Diamond's motto would be in full force: "We will." The stakes were high.

Immediately after getting off the ship, all troops marched to their transit area where they stacked their duffle bags. Then they marched with wet feet—due to the gap between the landing craft and the beach—for sixteen miles to the division concentration area where German aircraft made brief reconnaissance and harassing raids. They were assigned to V Corps, First Army, and were to relieve the 1st Infantry Division in the Caumont area where General Patton had come in and was in charge of the takeover and the Third Army. From then on Joe was in Patton's Third Army.

France was hot and dusty and full of signs of war. Towns were shell shattered; dead cows lay in the fields. Signs read: "Mines cleared to the hedges" or "Mines cleared to edge of the road." Artillery rumbled like thunder in the distance. Planes roared overhead. A heavy, putrid smell was in the air. Joe said, "The only thing I wanted to do was stay alive…and come home; I DID NOT like the Army one BIT; in fact, I hated every damn minute of it."

The 5th Division, First Army switch with the 1st Infantry Division in the Caumont Sector was made by replacing all who were there. It took six truck companies which totaled 290 trucks. Relief was made unit by unit with no changes in disposition; as much as possible it was position for position and weapon for weapon. Guides from units led replacements by covered routes to defensive positions they were to occupy. A "Red Diamond" man stepped into a dusty foxhole as soon as a veteran crawled out. By 14 July, the 5th had assumed responsibility for the sector. The 11th Infantry, which Joe was in, relieved the 26th Infantry, specifically. Small groups of NCOs and officers of the battle-tested First remained with the 5th for a few days to assist with the men learning about the activities of the enemy in that sector and about the combat, in general.

My father is walking behind an armored tank in a full-page picture in a Fifth Army history book. Hot-looking dust billows as thick as fog. His long-sleeved fatigue shirt is wet with sweat. He's carrying a wash-tub-sized backpack with a bazooka gun bouncing on top of it. His helmet has brown limbs and brush attached to the top of it; his eyes scanning the landscape look strong, resolute and vigilant. His first days began to click off with artillery duels, sniper fire and patrol activity.

Dad always included the Battle of St. Lo with his telling of memories of the war. He'd become meditative, as if reliving it, speak softly, and with what seemed like agony with each word. He said our troops and the German soldiers had been bottlenecked around Caumont, and they were preventing us from moving forward. He said there were three hundred small planes and more than a thousand bombers that flew in and dropped their bombs too short, killing too many of our own men. He said America's pilots dropped bombs in waves and almost leveled the town. He did not know why the U.S. air command went to such extremes.

In more detail, other records say Operation Cobra had been planned as a breakthrough effort beginning with a carpet bombing attack along German lines followed by a general offensive along the entire Army front. The breakthrough was designed to be made west of St. Lo, the key city and road center of the area, and to continue southwest toward Granville. The target date was set for July 22, but weather and other factors forced it to the 25th at eleven o'clock.

The 30th Infantry Division was assigned the task of taking the high ground, a ridge, just to the west of St. Lo. They accomplished that on July 20, thus denying the Germans of their prime observation positions overlooking St. Lo. With the town liberated, the major task for the 30th Infantry was to quickly move through hedgerows to overcome the German main line of resistance to create a wide breach. This would allow General Patton and his newly formed

Third Army to pass through and proceed southward toward Brest Peninsula. In the days right before the target date, General Omar Bradley and others were in England coordinating the attack with the Britain's Army Air Corps (AAC). It seems there was a disagreement concerning the direction of the Air Corps' attack and bombing. The Air Corps wanted to bomb head-on, perpendicular to the German main line of resistance as that would allow the least amount of exposure time for the planes to be targeted by German anti-aircraft artillery. General Bradley disagreed with that approach as he was afraid it was too risky, in case a few bombs were dropped short.

He demanded an east-to-west direction, parallel to the highway. The target date was July 24 at H-Hour set for 11:30 a.m. Everybody was ready including General Patton and his Third Army. A few hours prior to H-Hour all the troops of the 30th Division were withdrawn 1,200 yards to the north just in case, to allow for any misdirected bombs or artillery shells dropping short.

At fifteen minutes prior to H-Hour, the 30th Division artillery fired a preparation of red smoke shells to more clearly define the bomb line for the Air Corps. As soon as the shells were fired, landed and exploded, the red smoke began to disperse along the main line of resistance and highway—just as planned—then, a slight breeze from the south came up and smoke began to drift back towards the north. In just a few minutes, the red smoke was on top of our 30th Infantry Division men. When the planes left England, they were operating under radio silence and there was no means established at that time to reach the planes or divert the bombing. Thus, the high-pitched drone of the engines of over 350 P-48s followed by the drone of 1,500 heavy bombers could be heard coming from the north—not from the east as had been expected. Planes reached the target and rained down directly on the red smoke line and over our own troops.

Why did this happen? Why did the Air Corps, after agreeing to bomb parallel to the main line of resistance and to the highway, east to west, come in from the north? Who knows the answers to why this happened? But on that single day, 93 men were killed, 530 were wounded, and 60 were missing in action and later found buried in the rubble. Some reports even say the whole town was leveled. The next day a similar situation occurred. Some records report a total of 40,000 people killed in the effort to take the town of St. Lo. The next afternoon Joe's unit moved six miles northeast of St. Lo.

After that, Joe's group proceeded to the Vivre River and seized the bridges across the Maine and Loire rivers. After capturing the city of Angers—the main exit for the German troops fleeing the Brest Peninsula—they continued moving toward Paris and Fontainebleau.

During this time, Joe had an opportunity to go to the dispensary to get some help for his sore throat. He'd had it for weeks but there hadn't been a lull in the fighting or a doctor available. The dispensary doctor put him in a chair and told him to lean back. Then he put a tool with a clamp in Joe's mouth and cut out one tonsil and threw it in the trash. Next, he put the tool back in Joe's mouth and cut out the other tonsil. No anesthesia; nothing to deaden the pain. Joe said, "Then, I got up out of that chair and kept marchin' across France."

There was no rest for the Red Diamond unit. The days passed with frequent artillery duels, sniper fire and patrol activity. The enemy had occupied their prepared, positions for almost a month and its defense of the Caumont sector was well organized. Joe said he just kept walking, riding when he could, running, shooting, and dodging bullets. He said it was a good thing he'd learned to work and keep moving when he was young, no matter if he was cold or hungry, because that's what helped him keep moving under those horrible conditions. "War is hell, I'll tell ya," he later said.

General Walker, the Twentieth Corps commander, urged for more speed in the advance. In twenty-seven days, the 5th Division had covered seven hundred miles. They would soon be preparing to enter Germany. The Third Army's drive across France had outrun its supply lines. They had continued eastward, crossed the Marne River and captured Reims on August 29.

Joe's unit, the 11th Infantry, moving toward Corney, encountered German tanks firing armor-piercing ammunition and machine-gun spray. Just as our tanks reached a point about 765 yards from the brick factory on the edge of town, where they had set up camp, a German tank fired on it, knocking out all our tanks. This left the infantry unsupported, yet the riflemen, machine gunners, and mortar men of Co. B of the 11th drove the Germans off with sweeping fire, killing thirty-eight soldiers and capturing thirty.

During the night of September 12 the crossing at the Moselle bridge was completed. Heavy shelling continued during the night. Heavy rains made bathtubs of foxholes and soup out of dirt roads. Movement hill by hill continued. Then, on September 16, the 1st Battalion crossed the Moselle River.

Brief and savage hand-to-hand combat struggles developed as the Germans had not left Arnaville. Only the dead and wounded stopped. The bridgehead had been held, but at a heavy price. The troops of the 11th Infantry had withstood an average of one full-scale counterattack every five hours and numerous smaller harassing actions. The infantrymen fired until certain types of ammunition had been exhausted, and when full weight of enemy numbers reached our lines, the company's men stood their ground and destroyed the best of the Germans with pistols, rifle butts, and bayonets in hand-to-hand combat. Joe said he'd seen many things taken off dead German soldiers: mostly jewelry, rings, watches, cigarette lighters. "I just never could do that," he said. "All I wanted was to make it home."

The 11th Infantry spent five days overcoming the worst thrown at them yet by a spirited enemy. The Moselle bridgehead was now secure but at a staggering price. By September 25, 1,400 of the Red Diamond had been killed or wounded just in the Moselle bridgehead operation.

Next, they began preparing for the attack on Ft. Driant, which guarded the city of Metz on the west bank of the Moselle River. Throughout the whole Driant operation, the attacking battalions were exposed to heavy fire from all types of enemy weapons. The weather was rainy and cold, hampering both air and ground operations and increasing misery of the troops entrenched on top of the fort and in the area surrounding the city of Metz. The number of enemy losses was impossible to estimate with any degree of accuracy because the ground couldn't be held long enough to complete a body count.

Patrols were maintained, observation posts manned, and a constant watch kept on the existing enemy lines. On the 18th and 19th of October the 11th Infantry Regiment was relieved by the 379th Infantry Regiment of the 95th Infantry Division. Fires to disrupt counterattacks were used to great effect. Up until the relief of the 5th Division in the Moselle bridgehead late in October, the Division had been in almost continual contact with the enemy for forty-four straight days. Enemy artillery fire and aggressive attacks ranged from small-scale harassing missions to furious fighting and suicide charges.

All levels of the Division welcomed the chance for rest and reorganization. Supply and evacuation had been carried out under the most difficult of circumstances. During this period the duffle bags arrived from Monteborg by means of the quartermaster. This was the first chance for most of the Division to see and open their duffle bag and use the dry and clean clothing left in them nearly four months ago! Joe said he wore the same clothes for ninety straight days. The whole seat of his pants was worn out. He'd been able to take a shower a few times, but he'd had to put his dirty clothes back on.

On the 30th of October, the 5th Division was ordered to relieve the 9th Infantry Division in the Moselle bridgehead just south of Metz. A few days later, on November 2, active patrolling was undertaken in the front of the bridgehead positions with prisoners captured, enemies killed and some wounded on these patrols. This patrol activity resulted in several sharp fights. The 11th Infantry sustained slight losses when enemy patrols jumped small outposts in the front lines. In one such outpost Joe Barnes was on guard duty with two other soldiers dug into a foxhole the night of November 4, 1944. He had described the foxhole as covered with dirt and camouflaged with brush. Crawling out of the foxhole to "take a leak," Joe said as he stood up, he felt his left leg go out from under him and then he went down. His buddies in the foxhole heard the shot, crawled out, and dragged him by the shoulders back into the foxhole. They radioed headquarters and told them they needed support as Joe had been shot. His leg was shattered mid-calf. They took him to the main tent on a stretcher where they applied a tourniquet and started giving him penicillin, which had just come into widespread use as an antibiotic in order to treat WWII troops. That night they rolled out a wire runway in a nearby field for a plane to fly him to the 109th Evacuation station.

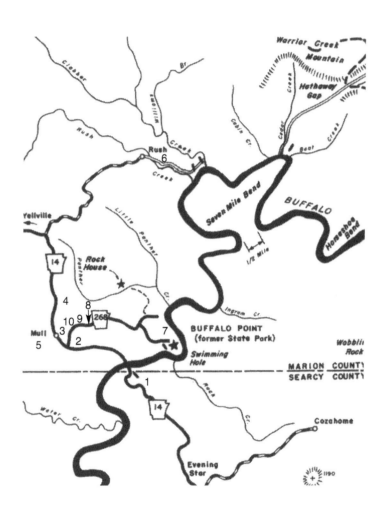

MAP LEGEND

1. Buffalo River Fishing Resort at the Highway14 Bridge crossing of the Buffalo River

2. Joe Barnes's original family homesite. In 1979 the house was moved across Highway 268 and then used as a rental. On the same property in the fork of the road, Joe built a large barn-shaped building to house the relocation of his canoe operation (when he was forced to sell his land at the Highway 14 bridge), which he renamed "Barnes Canoe Rental." Today, this is the site of Wild Bill's Outfitters.

3. Granny Bill's Grocery Store

4. CCC barracks

5. Home of Harrison and Alice Smith

6. Rush

7. Buffalo Point

8. Dirst Canoe Rental

9. Joe and Randi Connior property. Location of the office building of their canoe business called "Buffalo Point Canoe Rentals" and their home. Buffalo Point Canoe Rentals was originally located in the state park before the river became a national river, and was operated by Randi's parents, Louis and Harriet Pederson.

10. Site where the Barnes's family home moved across Highway 268. Today used as a motel by Wild Bill's Outfitters

Mary Willodean (left), 16 years old, with her twin, Evelyn, and younger sister, Mary Elizabeth. Spring 1935.

Wedding Day for Joe and Willodean Barnes (Joeseph William and Mary Willodean Smith). Married close to Buffalo Point in a curve of the road where Joe knew a CCC worker who was a justice of the peace. Celebrated that evening with the Smith family. April 7, 1941

Joe Barnes (left) and brother-in-law, Bennie Smith. Circa 1941.

Mary Willodean Smith Barnes and her daughter, Shirley Jo, who
is one year old. Joe saw his daughter once before he left for
WWII, and he returned home when she was almost four years
old. Willodean lived with her parents in Mull during that time.
Spring 1943.

Joe Barnes at war, in France, with the 11th Infantry, Fifth Army.
Once, after a lull in the fighting in France, Joe got a chance to
go by the field hospital to see a doctor about a sore throat he'd
had for quite some time. The doctor told him to sit down in a
reclining chair and lean back. He stuck a tool in Joe's mouth,
clamped his tonsil, cut it out, and threw it in the trash. Then,
he again told Joe to open his mouth, stuck the tool back in,
and cut out the other tonsil. Joe said, "Then I got up and kept
marching across France!" Circa 1944.

Mary Willodean Barnes (standing) with Virginia Callahan
who lived in San Diego with her husband, Jim. Virginia was
Willodean's first cousin and a life-long best friend. Willodean
named her second daughter after Virginia. Circa 1946.

Left to right: Willodean, Joe Barnes and Virginia. Virginia's
husband Jim is not pictured.

Traveling on a flatbed truck to pick apples in Yakima,
Washington. They stayed at Ramblers' Park and worked as
migrants. Left to right: Joe Barnes, Evelyn Smith McClain,
unknown, Mary Willodean Smith Barnes, unknown. Foreground,
right: Bill McClain (in overalls) and son, Mack Allen. Circa 1951.

Joe Barnes picking apples in Yakima, Washington. Bill McClain,
who settled his family there and owned an orchard for years,
said,"Joe could pick more apples in a day than any man I ever
knew. He was a hard worker." Circa 1951.

Joe Barnes at the original office building of his business,
Buffalo River Fishing Resort. Circa 1972-73.

A young man named Bryan Jefferson worked for Joe hauling
canoes one summer. Bryan said one weekend Joe had some
people floating from the Highway 14 bridge going to Buffalo
City, where their cars where waiting for them to drive home.
They missed the take-out spot and floated down the river
where they got out hours later at Norfork. They called Joe to
tell him what happened and asked him to come get them. Joe
told Bryan, "Jefferson, do you think you can find your way to
Norfork?" Bryan answered, "Yes, sir, I think I can." Joe said,
"Take that pickup over there and go get those folks..." Bryan
said, "Joe, there are four of those people and we can't all ride
in the front of that pickup." Joe answered, "I don't give a damn
where they ride; I want you to bring my boats back!"

Canoes stacked up and ready to rent at Buffalo River Fishing
Resort. Circa 1975.

Buffalo River Fishing Resort after Joe moved the original office
and built a new one on the other side of the road entering his
place. Circa 1977.

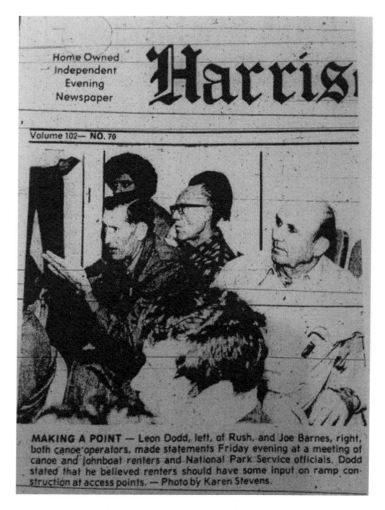

Article from the *Harrison Daily Times.* Jan. 15, 1979.

Joe Barnes (background) and his brother-in-law, Bill McClain,
fishing on the Buffalo. Circa 1980.

Joe Barnes in 1980.

This was the worst flood to hit Arkansas since 1945. Rainfall
exceeded 12 inches in 24 hours in much of northern and
western Arkansas. According to USGS reports, the average
discharge of the Buffalo River at the Highway 14 bridge was
estimated at 212,000 cubic feet per second, which translates to
1.6 million gallons passing by each second. In an interview by a
Northwest Arkansas paper, Joe Barnes, age 83 at the time, was
quoted as saying that when he crossed the bridge on December
2nd, it was "clean, pretty and blue as a bell." Then when he
returned at about 5:00 p.m. the next day the water was over
the bridge. He said, "I got my tools from my shop and took the
handrails off so trash wouldn't build up. I don't know how the
bridge stood what it took. The water was powerful. It looked like
the beginning of the end!" December 3, 1982.

So. Hwy 14 bridge today at normal level.
(courtesy of Dirk Helmke).

Same bridge during the flood of March 2008.

Our dog, Champ, enjoying the main swimming area at Buffalo
Point. Summer 2014.

Chapter Seven

RETURNING TO
SOUTH HIGHWAY 14

AFTER JOE LEFT FOR THE WAR, Bill worked as a secretary at the Soil Conservation Service office in Yellville. She loved dressing up, going to work; she loved being a secretary and having a paycheck. Since she was in high school, she'd wanted to become an executive secretary, even returning after her senior year to take shorthand because they added it to the curriculum the year after she left. Then, she applied to Droughn's Business College in Springfield, Missouri, and was not only accepted but also awarded a scholarship. First, though, she had to find a ride to Springfield. After nearly giving up, she found a man who was driving there with a flatbed truck loaded with lumber. Harrison decided to go with them, making sure she settled in all right at her school and at her new dwelling. The college found Bill a place to live and work for her room and board with an elderly woman named Irene who needed help with housekeeping and cooking.

The first Sunday after settling in, she cooked a roast for Irene and company who'd been invited. She told Bill, "Now, when they get here, you will need to eat in the kitchen; serve us first and then you stay in the kitchen." Mary Willodean didn't mind working, but she had way too much class and dignity to be treated as what she considered a second-class citizen. She hadn't known her job description included being treated as a maid who had to hide in the kitchen. Her only experience with company was to treat them with utmost hospitality. Within a few days she borrowed money from Irene and bought a bus ticket home, and never completed her schooling. "Besides, I just never could understand or see how Momma could do without my help," Bill said. She saved money to pay Irene back and mailed her a money order.

Not long after Joe left, morning sickness knocked Bill for a loop, forcing her to quit the secretarial position at the Soil Conservation Service Office, and once again finding herself at home helping Alice, whose housework and cooking had doubled since some family members had returned home. Evelyn, Bill's twin, and her son, Mack Allen, returned when her husband, also called Bill, left for the Army. Maxine, the wife of Bill's brother, Jessie, had died in childbirth when their daughter, Patti, was only two. Jessie, not knowing what to do with a two-year-old and grieving from the loss of his wife and the baby she was carrying, moved in with Alice and Harrison. Bennie, Leroy, Billy Frank, Mary Elizabeth and the twins, Ronald and Sammie, were still there. Bill knew her mother desperately needed help with the abundance of food preparation, cooking, laundry, and cleaning since it was like running a hotel.

The Smiths' new home, built when Bill and Evelyn were seniors, was full to the brim. It was nothing fancy, but they were all thrilled to have a bigger and better place. Bill said the whole time she was growing up and in school, she was never able to invite girlfriends home because their house wasn't much more than a shack. The new house didn't have running water or indoor plumbing, but it had three large bedrooms and a big porch across the front of the house with a double swing. The outside was painted white, with some of the inside walls also painted white, and others decorated with flowered wallpaper. Tall oak trees circled the house and Alice planted lilac bushes and roses along the edge of the front yard. Rough pasture covered with rocks and more rocks skirted the little white clapboard house, with a dirt path along one side leading to Caney.

Alice and the children made the best of what they had, whether it was daily chores, necessities like food, or clothing, or simply time on their hands. Ration stamps were needed for food or clothing and gasoline. Everyone got a ration book and neighbors would help each other out by giving or trading stamps. The little boys, Billy Frank and Ronald, helped with gathering eggs and worked some in the garden. Mostly, they managed to escape as much work as they could and find adventures of their own.

Ronald says that when he was small he had no one to play with. His twin sister, Sammie, would tell on him if she could get him in trouble. He spent most of the first grade in the cloakroom as a result of her tattling to the teacher, Mrs. Joyce. Then she would tell again when they got home. There were no boys his age living near Mull so only his brother Billy was left for Ronald to hang with and Billy had little interest in Ronald until he discovered how useful he could be. Ronald had to earn the privilege of hanging with Billy and one way was to let him push him on his bicycle. After pushing Billy up the hill, he would let Ronald ride down if he managed to jump on the back. If not, he would wait for him at the bottom. Ronald could depend on Billy waiting for him. If Ronald pushed Billy one mile, he pushed him a thousand.

When Ronald was older, his doctor told him his heart was slightly enlarged. He attributed this to pushing Billy. The heart of an eight-year-old just wasn't large enough to pump enough oxygen to the muscles for pushing Billy so the heart had to grow. Ronald attributed his good health partially to Billy, exercising him when he was small. When he asked Billy to get off and help him push on the big hills, Billy refused, saying it was Ronald's job since he, Billy, owned the bicycle. Ronald learned five things from playing with Billy that proved true his entire life. First, if you want something you have to pay for it (hanging out with Billy took work). Second, don't expect much in the way of rewards for hard work (Ronald could ride down the hill only if he was able to jump on fast enough). Third, he learned self-reliance because there was no reason to ask for help because you wouldn't get any (Billy wouldn't push even on the biggest hills). Fourth, don't ever give up (keep pushing to reach the top). Fifth, the poor get the dirty end of the stick (the owner gets to ride; the others walk and push).

One hot summer day Billy decided to make a shower bath and to include Ronald, who had never heard of a shower other than a rain shower. But Billy had learned about one and promised to teach Ronald. First, he sent him to find a bucket, which he did. Then, Billy sent him to get a nail that he found in the backyard where their mother heated wash water.

Billy punched a bunch of holes in the bottom of the bucket and hung it from a ceiling joist on the hallway of the barn. He then sent Ronald to find another bucket. Billy took off his overalls and sent Ronald to the pond for a bucket of water. On his return with the bucket of water, tadpoles, and frog eggs, Billy stood under the hanging bucket and had Ronald pour the water in it. He then sent him back to the pond for more water. Ronald carried water for an hour, but every time he arrived with another bucket, Billy's shower bucket was empty. No matter how fast he ran, he couldn't keep water in the shower bucket. From Billy's shower, Ronald learned another lesson: if you don't watch the small leaks, your bucket will always be empty, no matter how hard you work or how much you earn. Making their own entertainment and adventures came naturally for children raised in the country.

Constantly waiting for news about Joe made time pass slowly for Bill, even though everyone was kept busy. Bill's baby daughter, Shirley Jo, became the darling of the entire family, including Harrison, who carted her around most everywhere he went. Even without a father at home, she didn't hurt for attention. Often when Bill would not hear from Joe for a long time, the Army was good to fill in with a standard form postcard stating general things like "Are you okay" or "With all my love." Some cards were obviously phrases Joe wouldn't have used but, nevertheless, let Bill know Joe was still alive.

When Shirley Jo was two and a half years old, Bill received a telegram informing her Joe had been wounded in the leg and would soon be returning to the States. First, she was shocked and didn't know what to do or think. She knew this meant that at least he had survived and would be able to recover. She was thrilled Joe was okay, but grieved that she couldn't travel to be with him in the hospital. Having to wait for news was more difficult now, knowing he'd sustained a serious leg wound, and knowing he was alone without any family. She waited and prayed and learned more as Joe's letters became more frequent.

Joe was flown from the battlefield outpost near Metz, France, to the 109th Evacuation station for treatment of his leg wound. After two days he was sent to the 137th General Hospital in the United Kingdom, where he had surgery. His medical records show that he had a severe wound in his lower left leg with a compound fracture of the fibula, including shattered nerves. The operation date was November 15, 1944. A month later he was sent to Staten Island, New York, where he recovered and gained the strength to ride a train to Utah.

Military policy for treatment of wounded soldiers who needed long-term rehabilitation was to place them in locations as close to their hometowns as possible so family and friends could visit. Despite that, Joe was sent to Bushnell General Military Hospital in Brigham City, Utah, as it was well-suited for his particular type of injury. The 1,500-bed hospital sat on 235 acres in the southern limits of the city and became a state-of-the-art facility for its time, including a cafeteria that could seat a thousand. It specialized in hard cases such as amputations, maxillofacial surgery, neuropsychiatric conditions and tropical diseases. It was one of the first hospitals to use penicillin experimentally. Treating amputees and making artificial limbs were important specialties at Bushnell. An orthopedic staff cared for all fractures and deformities of limbs and joints. Other areas of specialty were neurology and psychiatry. Harry Truman, as a senator, once visited the orthopedic wards as he was interested in the advancement of prostheses.

Joe was fortunate to have the quality of care provided at Bushnell, but he still left the place changed forever from the war. Many citizens and volunteers other than professionals rallied to meet other needs of the soldiers, including job skills, morale, and mental health. Brigham City and surrounding communities were significant to the hospital's success. Citizens donated all they had in the way of time, supplies and money to assist in the care and rehabilitation of injured GIs.

Citizens of Brigham City donated recreational equipment such as checkers, jigsaw puzzles, chess, dominoes, Chinese checkers, softballs, bats, table tennis, Monopoly games, playing cards, magazines and books, which could be used by the sick or injured. Red Cross Gray Ladies, so-called because of the color of their uniforms, came to help soldiers by writing letters home, mending their clothing, reading to them, shopping for them, or doing anything else they needed. Some tutored them. Civilian volunteers taught occupational therapy and education classes. A soldier could obtain a high school diploma or college credit.

A year-round swimming pool was used for exercise and physical therapy. Dances, parties, and athletic events such as golf and basketball helped integrate soldiers who could manage those activities back into normal society. Celebrities visited to support morale. Bob Hope and Bing Crosby held a fundraiser at the nearby university and also performed for the men in the hospital. Shirley Temple once visited, along with many others with the USO.

Joe's convalescing at Bushnell Hospital lasted five long months. His days involved learning to walk again, although with crutches, and gradually placing weight on his left leg. He wrote and received letters from his family in Newark and from Bill. Nightmares interrupted his sleep regularly. He was ready to go home although these last four war years had changed him forever. For one thing, he'd developed a taste for whisky. He'd learned to gamble and play all sorts of card games to pass the time. And he was nervous and worried about the buddies he'd left behind.

During that time, Joe's never-ending curiosity served him well. When he first met people, he'd ask one question after another, as if he were taking notes: "Well, what'd ya think about that deal?" or "What did ya do then?" People responded well to him since they felt he valued their input. His interest was sincere. He didn't just question those who looked wealthy or seemed important. He didn't think more money or education or fame made anyone better or more interesting. Always inquisitive for a better, more secure life, Joe educated himself with others' stories and information.

In addition, fighting in a war impacted his inexperienced view of people. He'd seen his Army buddies take watches, rings, and other valuables off dead German soldiers. He'd seen friends and fellow soldiers mangled and killed while his own hands were tied and powerless to help them or make a difference. The evil side of human nature spotlighted in war was thrown in his face like ice water, which would haunt him and become a darkness he'd battle for life.

In the summer of 1945, Joe was released from Bushnell and traveled to Brooke Convalescent Hospital in Houston, Texas, to process out of the Army. His recovery time totaled 256 days. He was given thirty percent disability pension or payment because of his injury. He rode a train from Fort Sam Houston, Texas, to Marion County, Arkansas, where Bill and Shirley Jo, now three years old, were waiting, although they did not know an exact date or time for his homecoming. The war was over for him.

Arriving in Marion County on a hot summer day, Joe caught a ride from the train station to the Yellville square, which was the heart of all nearby activity in the remote little town of a thousand people. He wore the dress green United States Army uniform with a green beret covering his thinning hair. He came out of the service with a few medals: three signifying thirty consecutive days in battle, one Purple Heart, a Bronze Star, and Rifle Medals. He was not a hero in anyone's eyes, but his shoes were spit-shined, he was neatly dressed, he carried modest pride, and he commanded the admiration of a soldier's presence. His green duffle bag was light so as not to tax his weak left leg. A larger Army trunk full of other belongings would follow him later by mail.

Walking around the town square, some folks stopped and asked questions and were curious and friendly to him. "Thank you for your service," an older gentleman said as he walked down the sidewalk to greet Joe. Joe shook the man's hand and nodded his head. Others waved to him as they walked down the other side of the street. He wondered if some of them had loved ones who didn't make it home.

Catching a ride with someone, or the mail car, or a school bus was a common means of getting around in those days in northwest Arkansas. As he waited, like any hitchhiker, he looked around searching for someone he knew. When a school bus came in sight, he knew he could hitch a ride to Mull. It wasn't exactly a parade or the welcome a wounded soldier deserved, but it was the hope of going home to Bill and Shirley Jo that had kept him alive. He didn't care how he got home, as long as he got there.

He had been anxiously sitting and waiting on the stacked rock fence framing the court house to relieve the weight on his leg. Then, he stood up and waved for the bus to stop. The driver saw him and pulled over and braked to slow down to a stop.

As the bus slowed, two little girls sitting in the middle of the bus thought they recognized the soldier standing on the square. One was Sammie Lane Smith, eight years old; the other, Mary Elizabeth (Wig), twelve years old. Both were Bill's sisters.

"I saw this good-looking soldier limping down the sidewalk," Sammie later said. "I moved up to a seat closer to the front when I saw him sit down in the seat behind the driver. I've never been so excited in my life; I asked him questions all the way fourteen miles home."

When the bus got to the Mull stop, the driver opened the door, and told Joe to go first. Cautiously and little by little, Joe crept down the steps and then got his bag. Bill must have been watching the bus as Sammie recalled the screen door flying open and Bill's hair flying in the wind as she ran across the dusty, gravel driveway and fell in his arms. Sammie said she and Wig bypassed the lovers embracing in the road as they ran into the house yelling, "Joe's home!" to Alice, Harrison, Ronald, and everyone else they could find.

Later that night, the family and neighbors gathered in the Smiths' living room to welcome Joe back to Mull and to his family. They talked about the war late into the night with Joe answering questions about where he'd been, how he got shot, and about his recovery. Sammie, considered the louder, raw twin, blurted out, "Joe, did you kill anyone?" Harrison glared at her, "Hush up, Sammie Lane." Once again Joe was introduced to the Mull and the Smith way of life.

Chapter Eight

GRAPES OF
WRATH YEARS

*T*ROUBLE BEGAN BETWEEN Joe and Bill not long after Joe's homecoming. He had changed. Bill hardly knew the man she'd dated for three months and was married to for three more before he left for basic training, followed by four more long years, most of it overseas, during the war.

He'd returned with a limp, battle scars, and habits that would last a lifetime. He was having nightmares from things he'd seen and been involved in while fighting in France. Joe's transition to civilian life, to Mull, to a wife and daughter, and to responsibility for a family was slow and full of adjustments. Although he loved Bill and Shirley, he had acquired new and irresistible habits of running around, gambling, and drinking with little restraint. "I was just killed," Bill said. "He broke my heart."

One of the first things he did was buy a car, a 1941 Hudson, something that opened doors for travel to places and activities he'd never had before. Bill McClain, Evelyn's husband, also recently discharged from the service, was more than happy to accompany

Joe in his outings, which usually included partying for days.

Since Bill was crazy about Joe, she tolerated his new behaviors for a while, but it wasn't long until she got her belly full. "I'll show him; I'll take Shirley Jo and find somewhere to go and get a job myself." Some of her family members had moved to California to find work. She wrote to her cousin, Dee Nelson (my Great Aunt Rosa Dillard Davenport's daughter), asking if she could stay with them. Dee warmly offered her home to Bill and Shirley Jo, and said she and her husband, also named Bill, would do their best to help her find a job. After Bill and Shirley Jo arrived in California, Dee and her husband helped her find work in the C & H Sugar Mill in the town of Crockett, located northeast of San Francisco. Her job was shaping sugar into cubes.

"I was never hurt so bad in my life to have to leave Joe, and I thought our marriage was over," she said. The couple did their best to make Bill comfortable and to help her settle in to the new way of life in California. They knew it was a hard adjustment for Bill, she being a country girl who had never left Mull for long, and who was also heartbroken. It wasn't long before Bill wanted to go home.

When Dee's younger sister was killed in a traffic accident in California, her devastated father accompanied her casket on the train back to Arkansas. Since Dee and her husband were driving back to Arkansas anyway, Bill saw it as an opportunity to catch a ride back home as well as to go to her cousin's funeral.

When Joe heard Bill was back in Arkansas, it wasn't long until he charmed her back into his arms, and "We lived happily ever after," she later joked.

Joe found work anywhere he could to make a living for his young and growing family, since before long Bill was expecting another baby: me. They moved into one side of the Dillards' dogtrot home down Highway 14 from Mull, where they were living when I was born. Joe worked at the sawmill when they had enough work to use him, and also worked as a logger. Then, in 1947, the talk about building a dam on the White River at Bull Shoals became a reality.

Congress had authorized construction of the dam in 1941, but World War II had delayed the project. The purpose for building the dam was to provide flood control along the White River to protect farming land and to provide much needed electricity for a large area. During the spring flood of 1927, the river had crested at Cotter about 105 feet above the river bottom, lapping at the floor of the Cotter railroad bridge.

Before the dam was built, the White River was a major transportation route from Missouri all the way to the Arkansas River. It was easier for north Arkansas transportation to use steamboats and other kinds of boats on the river rather than the area's bad roads. From 1915 through 1927 floods became more destructive. The U.S. Corps of Engineers started work on Bull Shoals Dam in June of 1947. The White River divided Baxter and Marion counties where the dam was to be built, only twenty-five miles from Mull. Like Joe, many other veterans in Marion County, as well as men who'd worked in war-related projects, had been unable to find steady work. So, the Bull Shoals Dam project was a lifesaver for many families and for the economy of Marion County.

Workers from all over the United States came to work on the dam. It would be one of the largest concrete dams in the United States and the fifth largest in the world when it was built. Workers pitched tents to live in because there wasn't enough housing available for them. Near the towns of Flippin and Bull Shoals, employees begged for places such as a converted chicken house or any place that could be made livable, even though these dwellings would be without water or sewer. Flippin had no water or sewer system at that time, according to Jean Marshall in her book *The History of Flippin.*

Joe had no trouble getting hired to work at the dam. He worked there several months until his brother-in-lawBill McClain talked him into going to Washington state to pick apples where he'd heard pickers were making good money. McClain assured Joe he'd make a lot more money as a migrant working the apple orchards of Yakima, Washington, than as a lowly carpenter on Bull Shoals Dam.

Being young and strong, he and Joe were both up for an adventure. Plus the grass looked greener outside Arkansas. Plans were made in no time. Joe had bought a flatbed truck everyone could ride on. In addition to their clothes and other necessities, they rigged up two mattresses and a tarp for the road trip. Included in the group was McClain's family: Evelyn and their son,

Mack Allen, and five-year-old daughter, Alice Ann. By then, Mom and Dad had three girls: Justine, Shirley Jo, and me.

The day we left, Grandma Smith baked a bunch of sweet potatoes for us to eat on the way. But when we got to Yellville, Joe had to have some work done on a tire. While waiting, all the kids got hungry. Evelyn passed out the potatoes and as we ate them, we threw the peelings off the back of the truck to the ground. There we were: three adults and five children sitting on the flatbed truck loaded down with mattresses, laughing and talking, hanging off the bed, sweet potato peelings scattered everywhere. When Joe came around the corner from the store and saw the peelings, he yelled, "Stop throwing those damn sweet potato peelings on the ground!" He was embarrassed and mad. Mom said, "What do you want us to do? Eat them, too, or take them with us to Washington?" She thought it was funny, but Dad was silent for miles.

On the last night of the five-day journey to Washington, the weather turned cold. "We like to froze," Mom said. "We had two mattresses that we all slept on in the back of that truck." She said we used a bucket to go to the bathroom in when we couldn't find a public restroom. "I know one thing for sure: if it was to do over, I would not go on that trip," Mom said.

We moved to a place called "Ramblers Park" for migrants, who were then called Okies and Arkies. Mom said our cabin was the dirtiest cabin she'd ever seen. The floors were solid dirt.

Mom took us girls to the apple orchard with them while they worked. She would spread a quilt on the grass and tell us to rest and play because she had to pick too. Soon Joe and Bill were loading up the boxes with big Red Delicious apples. It wasn't long until Shirley and I were also picking fruit.

As was typical for Joe, he began to develop a reputation for being a good worker. McClain said Joe could pick more apples in a day than any man he'd ever known. At the end of the day, on average he'd have one hundred boxes of apples and the pay was eighteen cents a box. He had to climb a ladder sixteen to eighteen feet tall wearing a harness over his shoulders with a bag in the front. At the end of the day Joe and Bill pooled their boxes, turned them in for cash, and we'd go home to the dirty little cabin.

We hadn't been there long when I broke out with itchy red rings on my arms. When they didn't go away, Dad decided he had to find a doctor. He stayed home from work one day, cleaned up and put on his Fedora hat. I heard him tell Mom he had no idea how he was going to pay for the doctor's appointment because they were out of money until the end of the week. After checking me out, the doctor said I had something called impetigo. He gave us medicine and sent us on our way. Dad thanked, him, and as we stopped by the checkout desk, Dad looked nervous and worried. The secretary looked up at him and said, "Would you like for us to send you a bill, Mr. Barnes?"

"You bet," he said. "I was never so tickled in my life," he later told Bill.

Working through the picking season, Joe and Bill saved enough money to return to Arkansas. Bill and Evelyn decided to stay in Washington that year. Bull Shoals Dam was looking better to Joe now. Soon after returning to work on the dam, he'd moved from not knowing how to build a sawhorse to being an accomplished carpenter, then to being a foreman and running his own crew. He developed a reputation for being dependable, responsible and a good, hard worker. Before long, he was traveling all over the United States from one lock and dam to another, starting with the St. Lawrence Seaway. He was reading blueprints and worked as a superintendent on other locks and dams, such as the Hoover Dam and the Arkansas River System dams. We were living a nomadic lifestyle, but always returned home to South Highway 14. Dad was always learning, always restless. Mom said, "Joe quit more good jobs than most men get in a lifetime." If we stayed in one place a year, that was good. One year we moved twelve times.

Not long after the war ended, Joe and Bill bought forty acres at the top of the Buffalo River hill where it forks leading to the park. Then, in 1948, Joe built a little white cracker-box house for his family. Work was scarce for many in such a rural community, forcing Dad to go wherever he could for employment. Even so, that's where we always returned after those wild-goose chases to sock away money so we could return home.

The work on locks and dams was better than migrant farm work. Wherever Dad worked, he and Mom saved enough money to get back to South Highway 14. They always hoped that more work would show up somewhere close. Winters were especially hard. The little white house didn't have a well or inside plumbing. Joe had to carry water from a spring on the other side of the Smiths' place. The trip was about a mile, but it was a long way to carry a five-gallon milk can full of water on your shoulder.

Bill knew many ways to stretch a dollar. She never threw away fabric. She'd just re-work it into something different. She had a jar full of buttons she'd cut off old pieces of clothing: white, gold, black, tiny, large—every imaginable type of button was in that jar. When fabric couldn't be re-worked, she cut it up in small pieces to be used in a quilt. There were times when they didn't know where their next meal was coming from and that's when Dad's $30.00 a month disability check from the Army got them by.

Times were hard during the Christmas of 1953, and Joe needed new shoes. I was seven, Justine was three, and my sister, Shirley was eleven at that time. Shirley says she can remember feeling the financial stresses. Dad's shoe "flap-flapped" as he walked on the hardwood floors. He had been cutting logs to scurry up a little Christmas money for us. Shirley remembers having mixed feelings about things then: empathy along with embarrassment because she knew Dad was having a hard time about not being able to buy a new pair of shoes. There was a sadness hanging over us all.

Meanwhile, Dad had to make a run to Burley's Store, the local country store two miles from Mull. It turned out to be a profitable run. Burley messed up with Dad's change and gave him a $20 bill instead of a dollar bill. No one knew this for several years. Dad was ashamed when he told Shirley this story. But his need for the extra cash overrode his integrity to return the money right there at Christmastime. We suspect he paid Burley back.

When I was in the first grade, we moved four times. By then, at seven, I sensed something was not quite right about our style of living. I wasn't grown up enough to think we might be "poor white trash," but I knew everyone didn't live moving around from one town and one school to the next as we did. I remember feeling inferior,, especially because we were still using an outhouse at our home on South 14. I used to think, "No one will ever want to marry me; we have an outhouse, for Pete's sake." Plus, Mom and Dad fought and argued. Dad got drunk sometimes, and he could get mean, depending on what he was drinking. I can't remember the first three times I enrolled in the first grade. But the fourth sticks in my head.

Dad had found a better, higher paying job near Little Rock. We had boxes stacked up in our newest rental dwelling out on Highway 10 West, way outside of town. It was a log house in a nice wooded setting. We would be attending David O. Dodd Elementary School. We moved on the weekend before Shirley and I had to swallow another school change as the week started.

On Monday morning Mom did not drive us to school to register and introduce us to help us settle in. She simply helped us get ready to catch the bus for our first day, which would have to suffice for our orientation. She fixed biscuits and gravy as she was diligent to fill our stomachs. It wasn't cold outside. We were standing at the edge of Highway 10 when the school bus stopped to pick us up. We carefully stepped up onto the bus and sat close together.

Once at school, I worried about how to find my classroom. Shirley and I found the principal's office, and the principal took us to our individual rooms. My heart pounded as I looked for a way to get out of there. The teacher assigned me a desk and books, then went about her business. I looked around, frowned to focus and held my breath, enduring and bearing a flood of fear, and just wanting out of there. "How did I get here? I don't know these people. They don't know me," I thought. Finally the bell rang. Time for recess. I followed everyone, not knowing where the playground was. I walked around in the play area, which had lots of monkey bars and swings. I edged my way over to the outside wall of the brick school building, stood there and watched. I couldn't find my sister.

Another bell rang. I followed my group back to the first-grade classroom. As the teacher told us our assignment, she also wrote something on the board that I couldn't read. There was dead silence in the room as we first-graders worked. I opened my book. My stomach began to hurt. I couldn't read or concentrate. I was scared. I shut the book and tiptoed up to the side of the teacher's desk where she was sternly writing in a book.

"Teacher, teacher," I softly said, tapping her on the shoulder. She turned her head and looked around at me without smiling and said, "Yeeeeeesssss." She didn't appear to like students coming up to her desk.

"My belly hurts," I whispered in her ear.

"What did you say?' she demanded.

"My belly hurts really bad," I repeated, moving my head up and down for emphasis.

The teacher replied, *"Only pigs have bellies."*

Humiliation rippled through my chest. Gingerly, I tiptoed back to my desk with twenty first-graders' eyes following me.

My family laughed about that story for years. Mom would tell it, put her hand over her mouth, and say, "Can you believe a teacher would say that to a kid? And on her first day of school?" Dad would tell it and shake his head with his eyes squinted as if he were in pain. Mom would lift her head high and huff, "Poor little Jenny, that was no way for a teacher to talk to a kid!" Then, Dad would laugh and growl, "That teacher didn't think much of us; I guess we were like a bunch of pigs to her."

Dad's drinking and restlessness didn't subside during those moves. He was unpredictable. We just learned to look for signs that he was drinking and to definitely steer clear. He was a binge drinker. He didn't drink on a daily basis. Instead, he'd go for months without drinking a thing. He didn't just drink to get tight or buzzed. He drank until he was drunk, and he could get mean, just looking for a fight as he did once when we were back on South Highway 14.

Justine was eight, I was eleven, and Shirley was fifteen. Mom told us Dad had been drinking, which meant to stay out of his way. When he'd had too much, often he would pick a fight with Shirley, taking out his anger on her.

Shirley was ironing in the kitchen. Mom was peeling potatoes at the sink. We heard Dad's towering six-foot-four presence walking through the living room toward us and mumbling under his breath, "Goddamit, what the hell's going on?" Stomping his feet loudly as he walked through the living room, around the corner he saw Shirley. He started cussing and yelling at her about the way she had done something. He came toward her with his hand in the air as if to hit her and she immediately held up the hot, steaming iron in front of her. He backed off and then went out the back door off the kitchen, still cussing and angry.

Shirley and I ran to the bathroom to get away from him. I was still dressed in my school clothes. Mom came through the hallway to the bathroom and told us he had walked around the house and for us to run and hide in the woods behind the house because he was really drunk and she was afraid of him. Quickly, without taking anything with us, Shirley and I ran out the back screen door through the yard, behind the junk house and into the brush. There we stayed quietly, whispering to keep Dad from finding us. My legs were all scratched up from the underbrush.

A little later, we crossed Highway 14 and hid in the woods a little longer, listening for Dad's ranting and raving. We were still and quiet so we could hear if he was coming after us. We didn't want to go home. We decided to walk on down the road through the woods about a half mile to Grandma Alice's house, where we'd feel safe from him. We stayed hidden off the road in the brush and trees as we slowly walked north up Highway 14. We accidentally got into a bunch of blackberry bushes loaded with briars. I couldn't protect my legs in a skirt, but we had to keep walking. The briars scraped and cut my legs. But we kept walking and got to Grandma's house where it was quiet and calm.

We spent the night there and caught the bus for school the next morning. I had to wear the same clothes as I had the day before. My classmates looked at my scratched legs and asked, "What happened to your legs?" All day I had to answer that question.

Shortly after that binge, Dad bought a new brown sectional couch with a gold thread woven through the dark fabric. It was hard to stay mad at him when we were all so happy about something new that we needed.

While Dad worked on the St. Lawrence Seaway, we rented a beautiful two-story house on a maple-tree farm outside the small town of Hopkinton in upstate New York. He was a superintendent on that job and was able to get jobs for other friends and family who needed work. We had extra rooms in that big house, so we took in boarders. The boarder would pay Mom and Dad for having a good place to sleep and for meals. Mom cooked a big breakfast each morning, packed the boarders' lunches to take on the job with them, and then cooked a big meal in the evening.

Justine was in the first grade that year. She was a nervous child who could get hysterical in a flash. We all rode the bus to school together. During the day at school, often Justine would start crying, missing her mother. The teacher would get the bus driver to bring her home on the bus, no matter what time of day it was. Mom said she couldn't count the times she'd see that yellow school bus coming down the road early with one little black-haired girl in it.

A friend of mine there had horses. She taught me to ride and I loved it. She had a little black buggy and we'd hook it up to one of her gray dappled horses and ride all around the hillsides. One day Dad told me not to go riding with her. I don't know why he didn't want me to go that particular day, but he said, "Stay home." I went anyway. When I came back, neither Mom nor Dad were around. I went upstairs and found Dad napping. I paced back and forth at the foot of his bed. He said, "What are you doing?"

"I went riding with Nancy."

"Why did you do that?" he asked.

When I told him, "I just did," he came off the bed, got his belt and gave me three licks. That's the only time he ever spanked me.

Mom stayed busy cooking for everyone. Of course, we girls would help her as much as we could, which usually involved cleaning up the kitchen and doing the dishes. Mom never insisted we learn to cook or wanted us to do much but clean up the kitchen. She said we would have plenty of time to cook after we were adults. She had what might be called a love-hate relationship with cooking. She couldn't stand for people to be hungry and neither could my father. They had both grown up with extra appreciation for plenty of food to eat since they both had been in their teens during the Depression, and they both had come from poor families, both large families who grew much of their own food.

Mom had been cooking since she was young, and for just as long had been trying to get away from it, but the need to cook for people she loved seemed to follow her around. Our basic diet was meat and garden vegetables. When Dad would have a hog butchered, we ate well for weeks. Mom would make "cracklins" from the skin. Sometimes she or dad would make cornbread and add those crisp chips the way one would add onion or corn. I remember hog head cheese. Yuk! People really eat that. Usually it turned out a deep gray and looked kind of like turkey dressing. A neighbor once made blood pudding.

We ate beans and fried potatoes regularly, two or three times a week. Mom changed food up some to make it more tasty and interesting when she could. She'd roll the cut-up potatoes in cornmeal or flour before frying them, adding a little different flavor and texture to them. She put onion in potatoes. She made cornbread differently, too; it always depended on what she had. If she had buttermilk, she used it. If she didn't have enough cornmeal, she would add some flour or maybe even a little sugar to sweeten it. Her cornbread was always crisp on the outside and moist on the inside.

We also ate wild game. Mom made squirrel and rabbit dumplings just like she made chicken and dumplings. She cooked all the edible parts of a deer.

Beef was special. If Mom had a roast, she would cook it in an electric skillet on Sunday on low while we went to church. On Sunday we always had a big meal. That's when we would have pie or cake, which she'd make on the weekend. She made raisin, coconut, chocolate, rhubarb, blackberry, strawberry, raisin cream, and pecan pies, just to name a few of the desserts.

A lot of life revolved around food during those years: worrying if you would have enough, how to get it, how to store it, and how to keep it clean. Bugs got in flour and cornmeal. Meat rotted without refrigeration or proper care. Meat had to be eaten in a certain length of time. When there was nothing else to make a dessert, Mom would make a vinegar pie or a buttermilk pie. A vinegar pie sounds horrible, but when you are hungry for something sweet and tasty, a bite of the sweet juice mixed with tender homemade pie crust pops in your mouth. Basically, we ate what was in season, too. Dad used to pick wild poke salad, which was a green similar to spinach or turnip greens. When blackberries were ripe, we bathed in blackberry cobbler. Mom made jam and preserves, and canned quarts of berries for the winter.

She often wouldn't have much appetite by the time she got a meal on the table. Even so, she was a master at bringing it all together, somehow everything getting done at the same time. The beans would be boiling hot, the cornbread brown and crisp straight from the oven to the table. Potatoes fried crunchy and browned, sliced tomatoes, iced tea and hog jowl, bacon, or ham.

Mom's hair would be flying wild and sweat coming down her forehead as she plopped down on a chair at the table. She'd yell, "Joe, come on," right as the food landed on the table, and his chair would creak as he rose out of it and his big feet started to clomp toward the kitchen. He'd start "moseying" in from the living room. Mom never cared much about presentation or getting the little things, like salt and pepper, napkins, or butter, on the table. If she got the main items, that was good enough to her. As Dad and others at the table began to pass food, she might take a few potatoes, and then, as we would eat, she'd regain her strength and her appetite.

Mom loved good gravy. She could not stand the white gravy served by some, especially in restaurants. She wanted the flour to be cooked and even some-times almost burned before the milk was stirred in. Her brother, Jessie, used to say if it hadn't been for gravy, lots of people they knew would have starved to death during the Depression.

Gravy, like many things, can be made out of different ingredients, but good gravy starts with meat drippings left over in a pan, whether it's bacon, sausage, chicken, or ham. The greasy drippings give it flavor. Most of the time flour is added, stirred in and browned before milk or water is poured in to thin it out and make it smooth gravy. Back then, people used what they had, even coffee for liquid. If you add leftover coffee to ham drippings, you get what many love and call redeye gravy to pour over hot biscuits.

Mom made all kinds of breads. She made biscuits that had more flavor than most. She used whatever she had. Sometimes she added shortening and sometimes she didn't. She might use buttermilk or not. She might roll them out or pinch them off and into a pan. She even made one biscuit item that she called Johnny-cake. She poured all the biscuit dough into a greased skillet and slammed it into the hot 450-degree oven and cooked it all together, turning out one large browned cake.

We never had snacks. As a kid, I didn't even know what a snack was. We had meals, and if you missed one, you just got the leftovers—cold—no microwave to warm up food. I was so hungry at times, especially after school, I raided the refrigerator. Even a couple of spoonfuls of cold brown pinto beans were tasty when slapped on a piece of "light" bread and folded over.

Mom didn't have much use for a woman who would not cook for her family. No matter how tired of cooking she was, she did it because she loved the people around her. And, as much as she wanted out of the kitchen, it seemed to follow her around, even on our road trips to live away from South Highway 14.

In 1959 Dad built Mom a grocery store at the entrance to the state park, which was right across the road from our home. As was typical of Dad's style, the store was nothing fancy, just a cement block L-shaped building painted white, with a flat roof. They sold Esso gasoline, and Justine and I had to go out and pump gas for people when they drove up. Because I was thirteen, I was mortified and embarrassed that I had to pump gas, especially if there were young boys in the cars.

Mom had a big ice maker on the back porch that made marvelous little squares of hard ice to sell. Every morning, she'd bag up the ice. She had muscles in her arms that a man would have been proud to have. Probably her biggest selling item, though, was T-shirts. She could hardly keep them in stock. Many of the shirts had "I survived the Buffalo River" with a picture of a canoe and the river on them.

In the spring our whole family packed up for outings and went to the river. We'd take sandwiches, soap, towels, and clean clothes. Usually no one else would be at the main swimming hole in the park, making it seem as though it was our backyard, our river. A rope swing dangled from a water oak on the opposite side of the gravel bar. In the hot summertime, we spent many hours both lying in the gravelly sand and swinging from the rope into the green water. At times the river would be swift, but we all knew where the rest station was on the boulder-size rock hidden halfway between the rope and the bank.

Once, after lunch on a hot day in August, Justine was swimming to the rock after swinging from the rope. We knew the river was up some, but hadn't thought much about it. Shirley was standing on the boulder when she noticed Justine struggling to get to it. Justine yelled, "I can't make it!" Shirley Jo yelled back to her, "Just swim with the current; swim down with the current and over to the bank." Instead of swimming up to the rock, Justine began swimming downstream and over toward the bank. Shirley Jo managed to get to her and escorted her, gasping, to the bank. It was a close call.

When it was warm, it paid to live fourteen miles out in the country. Carloads of people from town drove to the Buffalo to spend the day or the afternoon. The rest of the year we were the ones who had to find a ride to town if we wanted to socialize, or go to a ballgame or a dance. But in the summers, the river was the place to be; it was ours and we just let others borrow it. We seemed to leave our cares behind, to simply rest, have fun, drink the fresh air, and enjoy the wet earth smells there.

Not long after Dad built the store, Mom was pregnant again, surprising everyone since she was forty-two. Another girl, named Scarlett Dean, came along in January of 1960. Some people wondered if having four girls might have been the reason why Joe kept drinking.

Without driving to Yellville, there were no other stores for people who were camping in the park. Also, about that time South Highway 14 was paved for the first time, bringing much more traffic to the area. Mom only kept the store open in the summers. She enjoyed all the people she met in the store and treated them with respect and consideration. Local folks came by just to visit. She had a piano in the store, so sometimes it was more like someone's home or a church with all the singing going on. She'd help tourists remember items that were easy to forget but much needed, such as ice. Since our home was right across the road, if someone needed something after she'd closed at 5 o'clock, she'd run over there to help them out. No telling how many meals were interrupted by late customers stopping by needing ice or an item for a child.

Owning a business that is open seven days a week, from eight to five, really ties one down. Many times Mom couldn't go places or she'd make one of us stay at the store if she needed to go. Uncle Pate, Alice's brother, worked for her some, and she hired other help occasionally.

The only curse word I ever heard Mom say was once when she wanted to go to her mother's house but it wasn't time to close the store. All the kids were going there, and Sammie was bringing watermelons. Dad was supposed to come down to the store and take over so we could all leave for Grandma's house. We waited and waited. A customer came and took forever to make her purchases. Mom was getting more impatient all the time. It was at the end of a week and she was not just impatient, she was tired. All of a sudden, she grabbed her keys and her money bag, marched toward the door and, totally out of character, said, "We'll just lock the son of a bitch up!"

By closing the store after school started, Mom could travel with Dad when he was working on a job somewhere else. If it was during her open season, she would move with him when she could get help in the store. The last place she lived away from home was in Jacksonville, Arkansas, when Dad was working on the Arkansas River System.

Dad got tired of traveling and living away from home, especially during the summers when Mom had the store open and she couldn't travel with him. About that time, the land where South Highway 14 crosses the Buffalo came up for sale. It was 1969. After much indecision, and even though they knew there was a possibility the river would be dammed or declared a national river, Joe decided, with Willodean's encouragement, to go ahead and see what he could do with running a canoe rental.

But owning a beautiful place and running a business on the Buffalo River were not good enough reasons to keep Dad from drinking. In fact, many customers brought plenty to drink while they were on the river. Regulars were never stingy about sharing what they brought to a "dry county." Part of the appeal of floating or fishing on a free-flowing river is the liberty to do pretty much what you want to without someone looking over your shoulder and the peace that comes from not having to meet deadlines. Many went there to simply get away. Freedom was the appeal and Dad fit right in with that crowd as he didn't really like anyone peering over his shoulder either, and he wanted to do what he wanted to do, often saying, "A man's gotta do what a man's gotta do."

The business grew fast, more than doubling in the first few years. Canoes were neatly stacked on trailers parked under the bridge. Buses with "Barnes Canoe Rental" on the sides, as well as pickup trucks, were neatly parked in rows. The grass was mowed. The air was fresh. Nothing was fancy, but all was in place and tidy.

In 1972, when the river finally was designated the Buffalo National River, everyone who owned property all the way up and down it knew they'd eventually be forced to sell their land. Sad but true. Dad decided he would stay at the bridge as long as they would let him. He thought he might not have to sell for years since he was on the lower end of the river and the National Park Service would start negotiating and acquiring the land at the headwaters first and then work their way down. He decided he'd move as many of his buildings as possible and build a new office building where our home was, up the hill and across the road from the store. One winter he built Mom a new home farther back behind the old house, which he moved across Highway 268 to rent as a motel. He was getting ready for the inevitable, and he would not waste one building.

The Buffalo was the first river in the nation designated by the National Park Service to become a national river area. So there was no precedent set as to how the surrounding land would be acquired and then managed. All the canoe haulers were stewing about how their businesses would be impacted by the government taking over. They knew the permits to rent canoes would be limited. There were no guarantees they'd be able to keep their businesses, as far as they could tell. All they could do was wait to see what would happen.

Early one morning I found Dad sitting alone on his office steps, head hanging down with his cap on crooked. He looked rough. He hadn't shaved. I sat down beside him and snuggled into his side, and put my arm around him. "I love you, Dad," I said.

"I'm just a sorry son of a bitch," he whispered, "I'm not worth a damn."

"Dad, that's why we all need a Savior."

"I need more than that," he said, very disgusted with himself.

"If you were to die tonight and stand before God and He said, 'Joe, why should I let you into my heaven?' what would you say?" I asked.

"I'd say He shouldn't let me in. By God, I can tell you one thing. I've tried to be a good person and do what was right and help people. But I know my drinking ain't no good. I don't reckon God ought to let me in, mostly because of that."

After talking a little more, we prayed together that God would forgive him, and he prayed to receive Christ as his personal savior. But that didn't stop his drinking. Not yet.

Chapter Nine

TRAGEDIES ON THE BUFFALO

(IN THE WORDS OF JOE BARNES)

*T*HATE TO SAY IT or even think 'bout it, but lots of tragedies happened on this here river. Some I try to forgit. One happened 'bout three miles above this bridge, close to where Spring Creek runs into the river. Not sure what year it was, but it was in early April or May. A man and woman and their fourteen-year-old son stopped by Joe Bennett's Canoe Rental, jest up Highway 14 from my place, one Saturday mornin' wantin' to float. Bennett told them it'd been rainin' upriver for a couple days; the river would be up and big. They said they didn't care; they'd floated before and they wanted to go. He told them he'd take them to Maumee, ten miles upriver, and they could float down to the main park. He thought they'd be ahead of the highest flood water since it'd rained way up the river. The family was with another couple who was floatin' with a different canoe operator, Dirst, maybe, or U. D. Lynch.

When Bennett let the trio out at Maumee, the river was big and brown, slitherin' along like a muddy snake. The floaters weren't concerned. Bennett told them to wear their life jackets and if they turned over, to git away from the canoe. That's what we always told people 'bout floatin'. You want to be upriver from a canoe so as not to git squeezed between the canoe and a branch or a tree trunk, or anythin' else for that matter. The other couple they knew had put in ahead of them. Bennett watched his three floaters start paddlin' down the river and drove back to his office, a little unsettled.

That afternoon, Joe Connior, another operator, owner of Buffalo Point Canoes, called Joe Bennett and asked if he'd he'rd of anyone drownin'. Bennett said no, but then got worried and called the ranger station at the park. They told him yes, that someone had drowned, but they didn't have the name or any details. Right away Bennett was afraid he knew who it was. Quickly he picked out a johnboat, threw in some tools, and instructed a couple hands to go with him. They drove to the bridge to put in and motor upriver. Bennett knew it was too late to save the drowned person, but he wanted to see and know what had happened and also git his canoe.

As they motored up the swollen river, park rangers in a flat-bottom boat stopped them, and asked Bennett where he was goin'. He told them. They said, "No, you can't go up there; there's been an accident." Joe told them he thought it was his customers and his canoe. He wanted to git his canoe. No one knows how to recover a canoe or boat in high water like a canoe operator. The park ranger pulled a gun on Bennett and told him to go home. What could he do? He left.

Joe Bennett drove to the hospital and met the father, who was in shock but welcomed Joe and was able to tell him what happened. The float had been fine until they got close to Spring Creek. Floatin' through a swollen rapid that zigzagged, the canoe tipped, and he, his wife, and his son were thrown out. Fairly close to the gravel bar, the father helped the mother git to the bank and then went back to help his son. The canoe was floatin' in the middle of the flooded river, upside down and sideways. The boy was hangin' on to the center of the canoe on the downriver side. The dad started swimmin' toward his son and 'bout that time, the canoe slammed the boy into a downed tree. The force of the rushin' water pinned him between the tree and the canoe. The father told Joe he knew immediately he was not goin' to be able to git his son out of this mess. The current was too strong and swift. The canoe had trapped his son against the downed tree at 'bout chest level. As the swollen rush of current pushed against the canoe, the canoe bent over him, crushin' him, little by little, moment by moment. Tuggin' and pushin' for all he was worth, the father could not budge the canoe away from the tree. The boy could not move. Tears flowed from his eyes.

The mother helplessly watched from the bank. The father knew that all he could do was stay beside his son as long as the current didn't wash him away. Slowly, the water rose to the boy's chin, then to his lips. It gradually rose up his nose; the last thing the dad saw was his son's hand raised in the water. This is the worst damn story I ever he'rd.

Bennett couldn't look at a canoe for weeks, he said later. He was sick 'bout the whole thing. Then even years later, a friend of his said, "I don't think Bennett was ever the same person after that happened."

Stories like this and the history of the Buffalo should'a made the U.S. Department of the Interior and the National Park Service value the canoe operator. They should'a talked to us before they came up with all their river regulations. When it was time to decide how they were goin' to take care of the Buffalo and keep people safe when they are fishin' and canoein', it seems reasonable to me that they'd want to know what we thought and had to say 'bout such. The canoe operator knew the ways of the river, how canoes and boats handle in high and low water. They even knew, jest like a lot of locals who'd been raised on the river, how to protect the river and keep it clean, and how to keep it movin' durin' low water. When the river would git almost too low to float and there would be places where you'd have to git out of your canoe and drag it over shallow water, it was a bad deal.

Joe Bennett used to load up a boat and float from Maumee down and find those shallow places. He and some friends would build little rock walls on either side of low places and fix them so that the water could only flow through a narrow chute-like gap. Then it wasn't long until the water rushin' through the gap began to wash out the gravel and made it deeper.

We knew, by God, what works and what don't work well on the river. Well, the National Park Service didn't ask any of us even one question 'bout anything before it handed us their "59 Commandments," better known as the government's prospectus. And besides all that, we were the ones who would be enforcin' the river regulations and rules, to some extent, or at least involved in it. It seemed like what we knew 'bout the Buffalo, how to be safe, and what to look out for jest didn't mean much to them.

The Park Service people prob'ly had taken some kind of class in college or read a damn book 'bout canoein' a river. They didn't ask our advice on one thing durin' those years in between when the river became national and before they took control. Jest threw us a list of fifty-nine rules to follow, didn't matter to them what was costly to us or reasonable or safe or tradition. They jest handed down their fifty-nine laws as if they were Moses with God's Ten Commandments written in stone.

After the river was designated the Buffalo National River in 1972, nothin' really changed 'bout the way we did business. The NPS started upriver buyin' what it was takin' over. We drove the trucks we wanted. We kept the same number of canoes we'd had for years. Every canoe hauler knew exactly how many canoes other business owners had. We used the put-in and take-out places we'd always used. If we wanted insurance, we bought it. I let my daughters and grandkids haul canoes and shuttle cars when I needed help. Didn't matter much how old they were, tell you the truth, as long as they could drive. Bill drove when I could talk her into it. But we knew change was comin' soon; when the National Park Service got all the land along the river bought up, they'd take over our businesses, too. Fortunately, buyin' up the land along the 135 floatable miles of river took years.

I can tell another story firsthand. This one happened in the spring of 1974, May. That's when the heavy rains and storms come. It had been stormin' and pourin' down rain all of one mornin', and I'd he'rd the weather report. The river was jest before a big rise flood. The word was that upriver it had been rainin' steady for five days. It takes a while for the Niagara Falls-like swell to move down to our end. I was on 'bout the ninety-third mile of the whole 135-mile floatable length of the river. Other outfitters close to me on this end were bracin' for the big water. I hadn't put anyone in the river that mornin' for this reason. Locals and those who know the Buffalo know that it's usually a tame, family-friendly little river, and jest lopes along, but it can switch to be a mean son of a bitch, I'm tellin' you.

Four women, who had never been on the river before, didn't understand this kind of danger. They'd arrived at the main park the night before. Two of them were from Little Rock, names were Susan Bolton and Jerilyn Nicholson, I found out later. They'd made camp in the park when two others, Mary Sparks and Morna Nation, both from Texas, drove in and started makin' camp. The four hit it off and ended up sharin' a bottle of Jim Beam. Later, they told how they'd started to go buy another bottle in a wet county, since Marion

County is dry, but instead they ended up jest goin' to sleep that night. The next mornin', they rented a canoe from Patterson in the park and rode to Maumee in the back of a pickup truck. Mary told how when she looked at the river at Maumee, she didn't think it was the same river as the one she'd seen in the park that mornin'. Before they left that mornin', the river at the park was crystal clear and she could see the gravel at the bottom. But the river at Maumee looked like a brown, boilin' cauldron. She seriously asked one of the pickup truck drivers if that was the same river.

Back then, floaters were put in the river at Maumee North by loadin' them in the canoe with the paddles and pushin' them down a bank. It was a muddy bank, kind of like a chute, where we'd jest shove the canoe and it would slide into the river. Found out later these two women had never been in a canoe before.

First I he'rd of them that day was when two men in kayaks took out at the bridge and walked up to my place. They asked me to call the park ranger station and tell them that they had seen four women in one canoe. Didn't look like they knew what they were doin'. Most people, at least local folks and people who know the river, know that even on a normal day on the river, a canoe should never have four adults in it. Rain had been comin' down in sheets all mornin', with lots of thunder and lightnin', and the river was risin' fast and floodin' into a demon. One of the kayakers said, "The river's becoming impossible to maneuver and swelling out of control. Something bad is liable to happen and the rangers might want to motor up and check on them." So I called the main park office and talked to a ranger to alert him of what was goin' on.

Chuck Brooks was the ranger on duty there. He was a veteran ranger who had recently been transferred from the Gila Wilderness in New Mexico (as he had been described in the *Arkansas Democrat-Gazette* newspaper). He knew not to wait for an emergency call from park officials. He and a park lifeguard, Mark Franks, got out their twenty-foot johnboat and nine-horsepower motor and started upriver.

We later found out that Mary Sparks and Morna Nation hadn't been on the river an hour when they'd tipped their canoe over and lodged in some trees. Someone came by and tried to pull them out, but their canoe wouldn't budge. The two were stranded in the trees when the women they'd camped beside the night before canoed by, saw them and paddled their canoe near them. The two women from Little Rock offered to rescue the two Texan women in their canoe. As the rain pounded down in sheets, the four had pulled over on the gravel bar at different times to take cover and try to wait out the weather. They didn't know whether to stay on the gravel bar or git back into the canoe and try to float on down.

After the third time they'd pulled over and gotten back in the canoe, they were rushin' down the river when they he'rd a thunderous sound ahead, like a rushin' waterfall. Before they could decide whether to take out or what else to do, their canoe slammed straight into a big willow tree.

Mary Sparks had been sittin' in the bottom of the Grumman aluminum canoe, with her legs stuck under the middle seat. The other three women were thrown out. They clung to the branches of the willow tree as the river current pulled at them to drag them under. Holdin' on for dear life, they couldn't resist for long. Mary's legs had been pinned under the canoe seat as the canoe folded like aluminum foil around the tree trunk. Mary was well above water at that time, even though her feet were tightly trapped under the crumpled canoe seat.

The park ranger and lifeguard were motorin' up the river 'bout this time, not far from the women. When they spotted the women, they first rescued Susan Bolton and Jerilyn Nicholson from the willow tree and then tried to free Mary's legs from the crumpled canoe. Chuck could feel the crushed metal against Mary's legs but realized he couldn't free her. He also knew that if the canoe could be freed from the tree, Mary would be carried under water and downed as long as her feet were pinned under the seat. The water was risin' fast and now up to Mary's chest; time was critical. Morna wanted to stay on the bank near Mary while the men took the other women and motored back to my place for help.

When they got to the bridge and found me, they asked if I'd contact a rescue squad or a crisis unit in Yellville. Shocked at the ignorance of this request, I told them, "Boys, there ain't no rescue squad in Yellville or anywhere around here. You might as well hightail it back up there and save that woman from drownin' yourselves." Damn!

I told them I'd round up some help and be right behind them. I had two hands workin' that day, Jimmy Morrison and Gary Docekal. I kept a johnboat tied up in the river jest for such emergencies. I grabbed a hacksaw and an ax as the three of us jumped into the boat and took off behind the two park men. No tellin' what we were goin' to find or what we'd have to do.

The river was floodin' fast. We ran over all kinds of things—logs, branches, pieces of lumber, dead varmints, and junk—as we motored up. When we got there, the water was up to Mary's chin. I had to carefully maneuver the back of the boat away from her so Jimmie and Gary in the front of the boat could reach her to see how badly her legs were pinned. The damn park ranger had gotten his boat below the canoe, where the water was rushin' over, and his boat had filled with water. "Dammit to hell, git out of the way," I had to tell them. By the time they got to the bank, their boat sunk. (The park ranger who sunk the boat was the one later described in the newspaper report as "a veteran of the National Park Service recently transferred from the Gila Wilderness in New Mexico.")

I saw right away what had to be done. First, I tied the end of my boat to a willow branch with jest e'nuff room above Mary to give Gary and Jimmy in the front of the boat room to reach under the water to her feet. Then they took the hacksaw and dived under and tried to saw off one end of the seat of the canoe. After a few tries, with the river water above her chin by then, the hacksaw broke.

I got kindly shook at that point and told the boys, "Do whatever the hell you need to, jest git her out of there," meanin' that they might have to cut her legs off. They knew what I meant too. They got the ax and were goin' to try to hack the seat off. Mary got frantic and screamed, "No, I'd rather drown than have my feet hacked up."

Then I told Gary and Jimmy to go under the water together and use both hands to see if they could tear out the seat together. They both took deep breaths and dived under together and pulled with all their strength. Water was then above Mary's lips, with grandaddy longlegs, bugs, spiders, branches, all kinds of things, washin' by her face. The roar of the river was screamin' in my ears. The third time Jimmy and Gary went under and pulled with all their might, I'll be damned if one end of the seat didn't bend e'nuff for Mary to pull her feet out. I helped her git in the boat. She was shakin' and freezin' to death. Her feet were bruised and cut up, swellin' big. She rode, shakin' and shiverin', cuddled up to Jimmy in the front of the boat all the way back to the bridge.

Supposedly, the purpose of the government takin' over the canoe businesses was related to their main concern with the river havin' too much traffic. Not sure what they thought too much traffic could or would do.

But that's why they had done a study years back on what the river could handle without hurtin' its pristine quality. Later I he'rd the study didn't really show that any damage was caused by a lot of canoe traffic. Anyway, that's why the government was goin' to regulate the number of canoes that each operator could own. First, I he'rd they were goin' to allow whatever number each operator had had in 1973; then I he'rd it was 1977. Rumors flew around hot and heavy.

Another rumor was that the government was goin' to divide the river into three sections, upper, middle, and lower. Course, I was on the lower section with other operators like Leon Dodd, who had operated in the main park for years until Mr. Pederson outbid him and Leon had to move down the road off park property. Every few years, people who wanted to run a business inside the park had to bid for it. The National Park Service gave the rights to the lowest bidder.

Another operator, U.D. Lynch, had forty-nine canoes. Mr. Pederson and his son-in-law, Joe Connior, had seventy-five. He also owned three hundred acres along the river right below Gilbert, planned to develop it, but had to sell it all to the government. Joe Bennett bought the Caney store, which had been there for years, from Charles Robinson. The store came with canoes. A few years later, Joe built a new buildin' for his business across from the Rush Road. We all got along fairly well, except maybe for Fred Dirst and his son, Russell, and wife, Mildred Dirst. But while all this was goin' on, we knew, by God, we had to stick together and we did.

The spots we drove customers to, for canoe put-ins to float, were mostly ghost towns, or old dirt trails with names like Maumee North, the 65 Bridge, Gilbert, Rush, Buffalo City, Highway 14 Bridge, and the main park. Of course, we took people up farther, such as to Woolum, if they wanted a longer float. People seemed to like a one-day float, which could take anywhere from three hours to eight hours dependin' on how fast the river was movin' and how much people paddled and how much they swam and dilly-dallied around along the way. From Maumee North down to where I was at the bridge is 'bout ten miles and then from the bridge to Rush is 'bout ten miles. Those have always been our two most popular floats.

My favorite is from Spring Creek down. It's 'bout three miles, a little shorter trip. The dirt road up there is like a washboard, and dusty in the summer when it's hot and hasn't rained. I don't know how all those people that live close to that dirt road survive the boilin' clouds of thick dust in the summer. Mostly we took customers where they wanted to go and tried to keep them safe.

Some say we canoe haulers was a rugged, independent bunch of folks. "Different," you could say, we's kind of different. Me and Leon was the ones to watch out for when it comes to drinkin' too much. Connior, he's a damn Yankee, but we all liked him anyway, even though it had taken a while for us to warm up to him and trust him. U.D. Lynch was some kind of man, I'll tell ya. Tall and loud! He could do 'bout anythin'. He raised his family right on Water Creek, down close to

Maumee, down there in the boonies. Bennett was jest a kid when he moved in here, started rentin' canoes when he was twenty-four. And, then there was Fred and Russell Dirst, who got their start at Rush, where Fred owned property right on the Buffalo and charged fifty cents for takin' out a boat on his property.

In November, 1978, six years after the river was designated a national river, the U.S. Department of the Interior sent a letter to all interested canoe haulers on the Buffalo. That mornin' I rode my four-wheeler from the house to the mailbox, got the mail, saw the letter from the Department of the Interior, and took it back to the house to read it. When I walked in the house, I yelled for Bill, "You need to come in here; we got a letter we need to read together." She set down at the table in the kitchen with me and I read it out loud. Best we could make out, they were callin' a meetin' of all the canoe haulers the first Wednesday in December. It said the meetin' was simply to help each of us fill out an application for a permit. At least that's what it said.

Chapter Ten

THE GRADUAL GOVERNMENT TAKEOVER OF THE CANOE BUSINESSES

(IN THE WORDS OF JOE BARNES)

WE MET AT THE HOLIDAY INN in Harrison, Arkansas, on the first Wednesday in December of 1978. Conference tables were set up that night, kindly in rows. There was fifty people or so there, I'd guess. Anyone who was goin' to apply for a permit was there. The people I remember were Leon and Josie Dodd, Fred and Russell Dirst, Mildred Dirst, U.D. and Almedia Lynch, Louis and Harriet Pederson, Joe Connior, Joe Bennett, Bill Houston, Mike Mills, Harold Gordon, Charles Newland, and Druscilla and Jerry Jefferson. If someone was to have added up all of the people who rented canoes up and down the 135 miles of river, it was said to be 'bout forty businesses. The owners who wanted a permit were there, I can tell you for sure, and they were there on time at that. I was there early.

John Turney, who'd recently taken Lorraine Mintzmyer's place, was the new superintendent at Buffalo

National River. Lorraine had been superintendent for quite a few years and knew our history. She was okay. They were all okay, I reckon. John Turney was at the front of the room with a microphone. A couple other park officials was there sittin' beside him. He had his grayish blue National Park Service uniform on. He was 'bout five feet, ten inches tall, brown hair, seemed like a nice e'nuff person. I'm not sure if he realized he was in a room with a bunch of grizzly bears. At least that's the way I'd call it. We were like grizzly bears smellin' some sneaky sons of bitches waitin' to rob her cubs.

"We from the Department of the Interior would like to welcome all of you tonight," John Turney said at the beginnin' of that first meetin'. Then he went on to describe why we were all there.

"We've invited you here to discuss filling out the application for a permit to have a business, including canoes and johnboats on the Buffalo River, from its headwaters to the mouth. We realize that since the river and land alongside the river became government property in 1972 and we have been buying up the land, you business owners have known and patiently waited to learn about any regulations the government would control and ask you to heed. I suppose it should be noted once again that the main reason for all these regulations is to protect and preserve the Buffalo River, which I'm sure is a common goal for all of us."

Then, he passed out copies of the sixty-page booklet of fifty-nine regulations they called a prospectus.

I began to thumb through my prospectus, which seemed as thick as a Sears and Roebuck catalog, not understandin' much of any of it. But echoes of shock was movin' around the room. "God almighty," I he'rd someone say. "What the hell," Leon said, lookin' up in confusion. There was lots of commotion, people all started talkin' at the same time, askin' questions of John Turney, askin' him what different rules meant. There were fifty-nine damn regulations they had listed. Mike Mills was wigglin' in his seat with his hand up, tryin' to git his turn to talk over the loud roar of the whole bunch. "So, you plan to permanently do away with the Ponca low-water bridge, which people have used for years, and the Maumee North access?" he asked.

"As far as the Maumee North access goes," Turney said, "the National Park Service has determined that there's a site across the river and down sixty feet that is just as good, if not better, than the Maumee North put-in place." Then he went on to say there was an archeological site nearby that prevented a proper launch and take-out point, and that the low-water bridge at Ponca was certainly considered a safety hazard durin' high usage.

"Does it matter that we'd have to drive three miles over a treacherous mountain that calls for four-wheel-drive vehicles if we don't use the Ponca bridge?" Mike asked. "Does it matter that the added costs for gas and more expensive vehicles and more employee time would significantly increase charges for canoes?" Mike asked. "I'll go bankrupt in one year," he said.

U.D. Lynch stood up and asked, "Does it matter that we'll have to drive thirty miles extra over a washboard

dirt road to put in a canoe instead of driving two or
three miles out of my backyard?"

Turney said of course the National Park Service was
concerned 'bout our expenses. He told us he knew
these regulations were numerous, but we would have
time to take the prospectus home and look it over, and
we'd meet again the followin' week to discuss the regulations. The application was not due until December
28 for any business owner who wanted a permit.

I reckon the main regulation that threw me the
hardest was the detailed financial information we'd
have to submit to the NPS and git approved before we
ever got a permit. They wanted to know 'bout every
penny I had. Damn, I felt like they wanted ever piece
of clothin' I had on, like they were strippin' me. If that
is not an invasion of our privacy, I don't know what
is. Jest ain't no damn reason for this. I've got a little
sense.

The regulations said the NPS would have to approve
the prices we charged, which seemed like an outright
interference with the free enterprise system. They
would charge a percentage, for a franchise fee, but then
private individuals could float the river for free. Canoe
haulers would have to submit annual financial reports.
The National Park Service would have to approve any
canoe hauler's employee and those employees would
have to be a certain age and have a commercial driver's license (CDL) to transport customers. There went
my freedom to let my teenage grandsons in on a job.
There went my lettin' my sixteen-year-old grandsons
put in canoes and pick them up and shuttle vehicles to

take-out points so the customers' cars would be there when the customers got there. The National Park Service was gonna reduce the number of permits from forty to twenty, sixteen for canoe permits and four for johnboat permits, and they were dividin' up the river into three sections:

1. Pruitt District, six operators, 420 canoes
2. Silver Hill District, five operators, 300 canoes
3. Buffalo District, five operators, 480 canoes

You might say Turney lost control of this meetin', with everyone talkin' all at the same time and tryin' to ask questions and figure out what the hell was goin' on. Shock, we was kind of in shock. Turney kept tryin' to 'splain that the National Park Service called this first meetin' simply a "workshop" to 'splain how to fill out the application for a permit. More than once he said, "The reason no news media was invited to this first meetin' was because it is simply a workshop." But to top it all off, they wanted the application filled out and turned in by December 28—jest three weeks away.

I went home that night and Bill was waitin' up on me. When I told her 'bout the "fifty-nine commandments," she was madder than an old wet hen. I jest kept muddlin' over all of it. I jest wondered if the Park Service had intentionally not talked to any of the canoe haulers.

The mornin' after the meetin' my phone started ringin'. It seemed like all of the local canoe haulers were downright outraged. We were all wonderin' what to do, how we'd survive with all these rules and changes.

In a few days the local banks he'rd 'bout the prospectus and started investigatin' and figurin' out that this was goin' to impact not jest the canoe haulers, but many of the local businesses and especially the banks themselves. Canoe haulers borrowed money from the banks at Flippin, Citizens's Bank, and the Bank of Yellville and the one at Marshall each spring for new canoes, boats, motors, life jackets, and vehicles, and then paid the banks back after the season was over. When our businesses did well, the banks did well.

A *Mountain Echo* (Flippin, Arkansas) front-page article hit the newsstands sayin' the Buffalo bureaucrats got carried away. For years the *Mountain Echo* had supported the National Park Service establishin' a national river. However, the *Echo* now says it must take exception with what they called a "slap in the face" by the Park Service. I'll never forgit that article because I'll be damned if that's not exactly what it felt like to me too—like they jest didn't care or respect us, like we didn't matter. The river was theirs now. That *Mountain Echo* article asked, "How can the National Park Service reach its arms outside the park into pocketbooks directly or indirectly of the citizens of Marion County and other counties of which the river flows? They asked, "IS THIS THE END?"

Then it wasn't long until the *Harrison* [Arkansas] *Daily Times* listed our major complaints with the fifty-nine commandments and all the National Park Service wanted to regulate:

1. The number of canoes each permittee could have
2. Put-in and take-out places
3. Shuttle vehicles must have seating at all times
4. Employers must maintain a current list of all employees to furnish on demand
5. Use of a three-part registration form, in triplicate, for each rental
6. Loss/damages would be the responsibility of permit holder, not the customers
7. No internal combustion motors above the Highway 14 bridge; below the bridge engines must be 10 horsepower or less.

It seemed everyone—canoe operators, newspapers, banks, locals—all agreed that even if we businesses got permits, we'd likely be put out of business due to the high prices we'd have to charge jest to comply with all the regulations. At least twenty operators would be forced out upfront; now, only sixteen permits for canoes were said to be offered on the entire river.

We were organized in one way. We asked for help every time we talked to someone who was interested, whether it was a barber, a business owner, a newspaperman, or jest a friend. And I can tell you one thing for sure: there hadn't been too many times in my life that I've asked for help.

I he'rd before I went to the next meetin' that James Patterson, president of the Flippin bank, was goin' to file its own lawsuit against the NPS to block the prospectus, as the bank said it was "stifling and too restrictive." The newspaper said Patterson felt it was the bank's duty to assure fair and equitable solutions. They wanted to file a temporary restrainin' order. Leon Dodd called me the night before our second meetin'.

"Joe, what do you think about the bank filing a restraining order against the NPS? Have you ever in your life heard of such?"

"We'll jest have to give it time, I reckon," I told him. "Let's go to the meetin' tomorrow night and see what happens." It was a Wednesday night, the second Wednesday in that December. Bill didn't go to the meetin'; she said she couldn't take goin' to the meetin'. But she starched and ironed my best white shirt like she always did when I dressed up. I wore a good pair of dress pants, my cowboy boots shined up, and a Pendleton wool shirt for a jacket, and of course my best felt Fedora hat. A bald head needs somethin' to keep it warm.

Mike Mills had called me and we decided to meet in the bar at the Holiday Inn. This meetin' would be close by in one of the conference rooms. Mike and I walked in at 'bout the same time. We shook hands, sat down on a stool at the bar. He ordered a Coors; I order scotch.

"Joe, what's going on? What the hell are we going to do?" Mike said.

"Hells bells, we'll have to hold our ground with them is all I know, jest do what we can and not back down," I said. "We may have to git a lawyer is what

I'm thinkin'. Maybe after tonight we'll git a better idea what we need to do."

"I might as well lock my door and throw away the keys," Mike said.

After we finished our drink, we found the conference room. There was more NPS officials here tonight. And there was reporters from newspapers all over Arkansas. I seen the old superintendent of the Buffalo National River, Lorraine Mintzmyer, and a few unfamiliar faces from the government. The room was set up different too. There was rows of foldin' chairs for all interested parties: newspapermen, canoe haulers, outfitters from White River, Arkansas. The Park Service officials had a microphone set up and they all set at a conference table at the front.

"Welcome and thank you for coming," John Turney said to open the meeting. "We hope to all come together and cooperate and work toward an agreement." He asked us, "What is it you all want for your business?"

Mike stood up and said he wanted the Ponca low-water bridge access. If not, he'd go bankrupt in one year. Leon Dodd said he wanted the Maumee North access and the same number of canoes he had before the prospectus. Someone, I can't remember who it was, asked, "How can you come outside your park boundaries and tell us what to do when we are not inside your boundaries?" In most parks the businesses are inside the park boundaries.

John Turney stumbled over this question and said as far as he knew this had never really happened before. But the shit really hit the fan when they started tellin' each one of us how many canoes we had. They had a number for each of us.

Russell Dirst stood up and said, "How do you know that's how many canoes I have?" Ms. Mintzmyer stood up and said she'd come out and counted them recently.

"I'll be dammed if that woman hadn't sneaked around without any of us knowing and counted our canoes," Russell said.

What 'bout the canoes that was rented? What 'bout the ones that ain't any good? What 'bout the ones that were somewhere bein' repaired? All these questions were asked and no one in the Park Service could answer them. Talkin out loud and whisperin' broke out everywhere, like a big wasp nest. We was all mad as hell now. The Park Service had crossed the line.

The next topic the NPS brought up was 'bout vehicles and transportin' customers. I'd hauled people any way I wanted to or could. If one of my customers didn't like what I had for them to ride in, more power to 'em. I'd load people up on a flat-bed truck with or without a license, or in the back of a pickup truck. It might be insured or not. It might have seat belts or not. Hell, I thought that's what the free enterprise system was. If people didn't want to ride like that, they could go find a better place or stay home, or git their own truck and canoes.

John Turney stood up in the meetin' and said, "No one is going to ride in the back of a truck; every customer must have a seat belt."

That did it for me. I come out of my chair and said, "I rode all over Germany durin' a war in the back of a truck without a seat belt. I don't know why I would be forced to provide one for people ridin' to a place to git in a damn canoe." It got quiet after that. Some folks were mumblin'. Turney went on to the next item.

Mike Mills, Leon Dodd, U.D. Lynch, and I met after that meetin' and decided we had to find a lawyer. We'd all pitch in and pay for it. It didn't really matter what it cost. We was in way over our heads; so much of this was legal issues, and some of it had never been tested or determined in court before. And, here they were expectin' us to turn in our application in two weeks or so, by the 28th of December.

We called a lawyer, Jerry Patterson, from Marshall, met with him, and he said he'd help us. We called ourselves the Buffalo River Canoe Haulers Association, or BRCH Association.

Members were Jack Coursey, Bill Houston, Gene Houston, Russell Dirst, Leon Dodd, Harold Gordon, Mike Mills and Noel Baker, who'd sold to Mike. Basically, we all wanted Jerry Patterson to be our voice and to help insure we'd git some of these regulations whittled down to be practical, and make sense to us, common sense so we could stay in business. Jerry Patterson could talk to Senator Bumpers and David Pryor and other local officials and lead us in gittin' pressure put on the government, the National Park Service, the U.S. Department of the Interior to make regulations reasonable.

We didn't want no more surprises or no more NPS folks sneakin' around and checkin' our finances or tax records like Ms. Mintzmyer had when she sneaked around and counted our canoes. Damnation! And, we didn't jest want to fall for whatever propaganda they put out. They said they'd put the Buffalo Park Service headquarters at Tyler Bend because it was a good place and central to the river. Well, they hadn't. They ended up puttin' it in one of Hammerschmidt's buildings he'd fought for and had built in Harrison that was plum empty. Tell me that wasn't politics. Why on earth would they put the central park office in a county the river didn't even run through?

Most of us operators understood and agreed with havin' a permit system, but this system they were proposin' would make it hard to make any money and stay in business. Mike Mills was like a loud voice cryin' in the wilderness 'bout Regulation 13, not usin' the Ponca low-water bridge. He said drivin' over the mountain three miles to Steel Creek could put him out of business, when you add the gas, employee hours, four-wheel-drive vehicles and all the extras it would demand.

The Concession Policy Act (Public Law 89-249) passed by Congress in 1965 outlines the duty of the Secretary of the Interior and thus the National Park Service to encourage competition among concession-aires (private persons and corporations) in providin' public services and facilities. At the Buffalo River these facilities are canoe rentals and johnboat shuttle services, although the canoe businesses are located outside NPS boundaries. This was virgin territory.

Jerry Patterson was the BRCH spokesperson, you might say. The group asked me to be the president, but hell I can't talk for a group. They told me people listened to me and respected me and trusted me. I asked Mike Mills if he would lead us.

Most of the time our lawyer spoke to the press for us all. Our strategy was to be reasonable. Jerry told the press that some of the fifty-nine regulations simply were not practical. And many of us were riled up mostly because we hadn't been given a chance to even present our opinions. Honestly, the way the National Park Service had handled this whole thing was kind of like Moses comin' down from the mountain with Ten Commandments and throwin' them at us. Hells bells, who wouldn't git mad? Jest all of a sudden the Buffalo River has been kidnapped from us and we can't use it anymore? This was our land. Leastways it had been our land. Maybe these services, our services they called concessionaires, are more important than they gave us credit. We'd become part of the enforcement of these rules, seemed to me like, and we could advise the NPS and work with them. What would they do without us?

How on earth had they divided up the river? How did they select access points? Not to mention regulatin' the type of vehicle we could use and what did they know 'bout replacin' damaged equipment?

In mid-December, the operators asked for an extension of the application deadline of December 28. Some wanted it delayed for a year, but John Turney told the *Harrison Daily Times* that prob'ly no date change would be made. Turney said the NPS must protect and preserve the Buffalo River. He said we all had to follow Occupational Safety and Health Administration (OSHA) standards for the benefit of both the public and the canoe operator. The concessionaire must be financially able to provide services for the public, which was the reason for the detailed and involved financial application.

In the meantime, James Patterson, president of Citizen's Bank and Trust in Flippin, Arkansas, was proposin' to block the December deadline for applications and implementin' new regulations proposed by the NPS. He felt it was the bank's duty to assure fair and equitable solutions as he was concerned 'bout economic impact in Marion County and the other counties affected.

Citizen's Bank and Trust called a meetin' with fourteen local canoe haulers to git our input and our backin' on their legal proceedin's. Some operators were afraid the NPS would git all fired up and mad if we was supportin' an injunction by the bank to stop the prospectus. Some were even afraid of retribution. Leon Dodd stood up and said, "We don't want it to get to the point where they close us off and give the canoes to some turkey from Chicago." Another asked, "Can they close the river down and keep us out if the banks file an injunction?"

James Patterson said, "Right now, they are God and can do anything they want to. Or at least they think they are." We all ended up givin' the Flippin bank our consent to go ahead with the lawsuit. It felt good to be asked 'bout things, instead of jest handed the Fifty-nine Commandments. The National Park Service went on to appoint four different committees to come up with more practical regulations to present to the court.

The *Arkansas Democrat-Gazette* reported that our area could lose $500,000 in income if they got rid of twenty-four canoe businesses. The bank contended that the fifty-nine regulations governin' the permit system were arbitrary and capricious, and were drafted intentionally without public comment and would take business away from the operators without just compensation.

Joe Villines, a lawyer from Harrison, went ahead and filed a restrainin' order against the National Park Service and the Department of the Interior. The hearin' was in Fayetteville on December 28th, which was the day we were supposed to turn in our applications and three weeks after the first meetin'. They called eight witnesses. James Patterson testified 'bout a third of us canoe haulers took loans from him and how we could default dependin' on the fifty-nine regulations. Paul Lingle from Ozark Mountain Region Promotion Association testified that the fifty-nine regulations could cause a 50 percent reduction in tourism. Jerry Patterson, our lawyer, testified that twenty-four canoe businesses would be cut, goin' from forty to sixteen, and it was based on a study of the river's capacity years ago—jest not practical.

And, the NPS hadn't sought one local canoe hauler's input or opinion 'bout any of the regulations. This impacted morale and popular opinion 'bout the government's role. Mike Mills testified he'd go out of business in one year due to limitations from not bein' able to use the Ponca low-water bridge. Much of the unrest stemmed from the fact that none of the businessmen were asked to present their opinions of the fifty-nine commandments.

They extended the deadline to January 15, 1979. Then the BRCH Association decided to request a meetin' with Dale Bumpers, and he agreed to meet on January 4th. We now had a deadline in two weeks and I can tell you one thing for sure, we needed help, by God. We met with Jerry Patterson first, all of us, and talked 'bout how to handle this meetin' with Senator Bumpers. We was jest gonna try to be reasonable and stick with the facts. What else could we do that would help?

Surely, common sense could make some kind of difference. But then again, maybe not, when you're dealin' with the gov'ment. Since Bumpers was fixin' to be Chairman of the National Parks Subcommittee when Congress reconvened on January 15, this situation was in his area. I talked to Leon and U.D. on the phone the night before we were drivin' to Little Rock for the meetin'. I'd met with Bumpers before once when he came up to float the Buffalo. Nice e'nuff. I was fairly hopeful he could help us. He could at least talk to the newspapers and stir up the public. That had helped us before to git people involved.

The NPS had kept askin' us in the meetings, "What do you want?" We were prepared to tell Senator Bumpers what we thought was reasonable. I got up early, met Jerry Patterson and the others in Marshall, and we all rode up together. It was a freezin' cold January mornin'. We drove straight to the Capitol in Little Rock. He thanked us for comin' and Jerry told him we needed his help, and hoped he would talk to those folks at the NPS and state our case. The paperwork outlined in the prospectus would take a full-time secretary. That's one big thing we wanted was less paperwork, and we wanted to keep the number of canoes we had. We wanted the deadline extended to be able to talk through the reasonableness of each of the fifty-nine rules. And we wanted, by God, to be he'rd.

After our meeting, he told the *Harrison Daily Times* he would ask for a six-month postponement of the proposed fifty-nine regulations to allow for extensive consultations between the operators and the Park Service. He told them the fifty-nine rules were "downright abusive." "The whole thing needs to go back to the drawing board," he said. John Turney said the Director of Concessions in Washington, D.C. would have the final say on whether or not to postpone meetings and deadline dates for the regulations to take effect. Bumpers had stated he found most of the operators' complaints legitimate, and the regulations would force the operators to assume burdensome and unnecessary expenses and bear responsibility for all equipment damage and loss. He told them our contracts would be terminated at the will of the park superintendent and our paperwork would be endless. "Everybody wants to preserve the Buffalo River, but to force long-time operators with perfect sanitary records out of business because of downright abusive rules is unacceptable," he stated to the papers.

After Bumpers met with NPS officials, they called for a meetin' with us on January 15. We listed our wishes for the total number of canoes on the river, for put-in points, charges for fees, types of vehicles we could use, motor size on johnboats, how to pay for damaged equipment, among other rules. Irene Samuels from Bumpers' staff was there along with Lorraine Mintzmyer, former BNR Superintendent, John Turney, and John Welch, the present Chief Ranger at BNR.

Lorraine told us all commercial canoe and johnboat operators in business in 1973 would be grandfathered in and offered a permit. They was tryin' to hold operator numbers to 1973 amount and canoe numbers to 1977 number of 1,200 on the whole river. At this meetin' the deadline for the application was moved to April 15th to go into effect on October 31, 1980.

We had one more meetin' after that one with jest a few operators: Mike Mills, Bill Houston, Leon Dodd, Harold Gordon, Charles Newland from White River, and our lawyer, Jerry Patterson. At this meetin' we were able to git a few more things we wanted. They added the North Maumee access but not the Ponca low water bridge. They increased outfitters from sixteen to twenty-four and they upped the number of canoes overall to 1,250.

In April we had the final meetin' and they passed out the applications to be one of twenty-four permit holders and gave us sixty to ninety days to git it filled out.

NPS adjusted many of the regulations. Like I said, we got twenty-four permits for canoe operators, instead of sixteen like they'd first said. We got 1,250 canoes on the whole river, and they upped the access

points to twelve. They deleted the trash bag require-
ment. Said other access points would be added. They
allowed open vehicles. Damn! The trailer regulations
was changed some and only had to have two paddles
per canoe, instead of three.

We gave it our best. Some say we canoe haulers
didn't git much after all, that the NPS knew what they
was gonna do before they even sent out the prospectus.
Some say they gave us the ridiculous list of regulations
to distract us from the fact they were takin' over our
river. Maybe so. I reckon I jest did what we could.
Fought the rules we could. A man's gotta do what a
man's gotta do. I had to start thinkin' 'bout movin'
my business up the river hill, across the highway from
Bill's store. I still had forty acres there. My land.

Some say our grandkids will never know the river
we knew. These are people who knew the river. Fishin'
is not much good any more. Fish can't nest and spawn
without bein' disturbed and interrupted. Hundreds of
canoes float down some summer days. It's like an interstate highway. Even the route and the channel of
the river has been disturbed by the changes. Some
locals say the NPS has ruined the river. No longer can
you leave the city and find as much freedom and stillness. Some of the things locals say: "It's not and never
will be the same river."

"The Buffalo River is gone."

Epilogue

In 1991, Bill Scruggs, a businessman from Mississippi, while sitting in a doctor's office picked up an
Outdoor Life magazine. In the classifieds was a tiny ad
which read, FOR SALE: *Buffalo River Canoe Outfitters*.
He called the number and later drove to Arkansas
where he met the owners, Russell and Mildred Dirst,
who told him the situation and what they had for sale.
They owned the canoe permits and equipment which
they'd bought as the old Barnes Canoe Rental business on the court house steps when it had been auc-
tioned off by the bank. Unfortunately, when Joe sold
the business to one of his daughters, his son-in-law,
and another couple, they lost it after operating it for
only a few years.

Mr. Dirst was operating his original business from
a store on Highway 268 about two miles from Buffalo
Point, and they were running Barnes Canoe Rental out
of a different location, closer to South Highway 14. Bill
Scruggs told Russell, "Well, if I bought the business,
I'd want the property up at the intersection where you
turn off Highway 14. I like the way that property sits
and where it's located for a business."

"Yeah, but that's ole Joe Barnes's land and he's not
gonna sell it," Mr. Dirst said. "Joe wouldn't part with
that place for love nor money." Russell and Mildred
told Bill that Joe was renting the barn-shaped build-

ing he'd built on that location when he was forced to sell by the Federal Government and moved up the hill from the river, and his wife, Willodean ran the grocery store across the road.

Afterward, Bill said goodbye to Mildred and Russell, and left to find Joe Barnes. He drove the short distance to Willodean's store at the corner of Highway 268 and Highway 14. When he walked through the door, "That was the first time I ever laid eyes on Joe," Bill told me during an interview years later. "Joe was sitting on top of the counter with his long legs and big feet dangling and his hat cocked sideways, and Willodean was sitting on the couch quilting."

Bill looked at the man he'd never met and said, "I'm looking for Joe Barnes."

"Whatcha wont with hem?" Joe asked indifferently.

"Well, I want to talk to him."

"Well, that's me," Joe said.

Bill went over and shook hands with him, introduced himself, and told him where he was from. Bill looked Joe square in the eye and said, "I want to buy this property across the road."

Well, it ain't for sale," Joe quickly replied. Bill stood around and made small talk for awhile trying to get on Joe's good side. "He was not overly friendly," Scruggs told me with a sigh, adding, "You know how Joe could be." Despite that, Bill kept struggling to make conversation with the man who didn't seem interested, finally coming up with, "You know, I don't know much about the country around the river here; how about if you showed me around, took me to some of the key spots?"

Joe said, "Okay, let's go."

They took the shortcut down by Alice Smith's old home place on the way to Maumee. Next, they went to Rush, South Maumee, and Spring Creek. During the drive, Bill told Joe how he'd like to put the business back together by buying the land, and the barn-shaped building from him and then the permits and all the equipment from Russell and Mildred Dirst. He said he'd like to run it from the same location where Joe had last run his business.

When they returned well after dark, Willodean came out of the store and said to Joe, "Where have you been so long out after dark and with a man you've never seen before in your life?" She was not happy.

"It's kind of funny how it all turned out," Bill said later. "I lived in Mississippi and had gotten tired of the businesses I owned." He said that someone was interested in buying his stores and had made an offer, which he'd turned down, but kept thinking about selling. "I'd just kept saying no, no, no..." he recalled.

"I told Joe again how I wanted to buy the old Barnes Canoe Rental and his property with the buildings and put it all back together, and how I'd like to operate it," Bill said. "The whole time I was explaining this to him, he didn't say a word. He didn't indicate one thing that made me think he would consider selling to me. But, later, when Joe got out of the truck, he slammed the door and stuck his head back through the window and said, 'Where you going? You ain't got a place to stay tonight. Too late to go anywhere. Just stay here,' and then he handed me a key to his apartment above the office.

"I knew I was in then," Bill said with a grin.

Sooner or later all the people who owned land connecting to the Buffalo had to sell to the government. Joe sold in 1980 and moved up the river hill across the road from Willodean's store. He moved everything—johnboats, canoes, trucks, trailers, cabins, and his office building, managing to find a use for it all. He relocated the family's little cracker-box house across the road between Willodean's grocery store and Joe Connier's house on the road leading to Buffalo Point, and rented it as a motel. After moving the house, he used the same site to build a large barn-shaped building for an office and a shop behind it to house trucks, trailers, and equipment. Then, on the back side of the hill, facing the river, he built a large, rock style ranch home for his family.

I'm not sure the canoe business held the same pleasure for Joe after he moved it away from the river, since he sold it only a few years later. His youngest daughter, Scarlett, remembers him drinking more during that time and said he seemed sad. She also remembers him saying, "You can't put a price on the priceless."

After he sold the business, he simply rented cabins he'd relocated here and there, made furniture (mostly for his girls) and took care of his property. Willodean struggled with the loss of the canoe business, which she desperately wanted to stay in the family. She wrote in a journal, "I guess Joe would have sold me if he could have found a buyer," meaning the man was restless and invited change.

Just as there were different opinions about what to do with the Buffalo before it became a national river, there are different opinions about how the river has been impacted by government control of it. Let me emphasize, I am not an authority on this subject, and the truth is that this subject is passionately debated by many. Still, one fact many agree on is that today the river experience is different than it was before 1972. Over a million people visit the Buffalo yearly, either canoeing, hiking, riding the trails, swimming, camping—or a combination of all of the above.

The people who support the National Park Service control of the river say it is better off now because no one can buy and build along the river, therefore preventing pollution and eyesores, which would blot the landscape. The NPS monitors nearby industry which can cause pollution as was recently witnessed in the battle over allowing pig farms close to the river watershed. Instead, they promote building horse trails and hiking trails free for all to use. There are no private fences to block people from using trails anywhere. The river is policed and rules are enforced, just as if it were a city. When the river rises, the NPS regulates who can float and who can't; all the way from allowing inexpe-

rienced floaters on the river to closing it completely.
They have added campsites, bath houses, rock retaining walls, tourist information centers, and entertainment, such as educational lectures. The NPS has made
many improvements and they are committed to pro-
tecting the river and the land.

According to one knowledgeable park ranger, there
are many other facts regarding ways that the NPS benefits the Buffalo. For one, the quality of the water is
closely monitored. The Park Service also preserves and
protects cultural resources such as natural features
like caves and tributaries alongside the river. There's a
better understanding of flora and fauna and, thus, they
are better protected. There can be economic benefits
to local communities and businesses from national
exposure. Often, although not always, there is better
access to publicly owned lands.

In addition, the NPS provides some preservation of
history in displays at park ranger offices, such as at
Tyler Bend. People visit and see pictures of old houses
and farms, and often one can hear someone say something like, "I knew him," or "That's my grandfather's
old place." Generally speaking, some believe there is
usually better, longterm protection of the river and the
watershed due to NPS care.

Then again you have the folks who say, "The
Buffalo River will never be the same; it's an interstate
highway for canoes now." Josie Dodd, who owned a
canoe service close to Buffalo Point said, at the age of
eighty, "I'm still mad that the Department of Interior
forced us to sell our land." She added that she went

to every NPS meeting regarding the prospectus, with her husband Leon. Many who used to fish the river say you could count on going fishing there and catching more than enough fish for your family's supper. No more. Some people are of the opinion that now the fish can't nest because there's too much traffic and people pollution.

Some knowledgeable, local folks say the canoe operators will all eventually have to sell because they can't make money renting canoes since the NPS took over and imposed so many costly regulations with regards to types of insurance, employee ages, and so on. In addition, they have to pay a percentage to the NPS on each canoe rented and related revenue. Now their overhead is just too darn high say the locals who also feel they can't charge enough per canoe to make up for the costs of the regulations. Many of the operators have found other sources of income, such as cabin rentals, horseback rides, firewood sales, and zip lines.

Charles Newland, owner of Newland's Trout Fishing in Lakeview, Arkansas, says much has changed about fishing and floating in the last few years, but not all of the change is due to the NPS regulations. The tradition of camping on the river bank is different. People like to come back to a cozy, comfortable room with Internet access and flatscreen televisions. For years in April, May, and June the majority of his business was fishing trips on the Buffalo. He'd pick up people who flew into the Flippin or Little Rock airports. He remembers having boats stacked up like cords of wood, ready to load and put in the Buffalo.

However, the impact of the NPS regulations is reflected by the following instance. Not too long ago, Charles picked up five men from Kansas City at the Flippin airport for a five-day float on the Buffalo, but the river was closed by the NPS to even experienced floaters because it was up ten feet. Charles says, "That's not necessary if you are in a flat bottom boat with a motor." His customers had to leave without ever getting on the river. He adds, "It feels like someone is constantly looking over your shoulder." Years ago the majority of his spring business was on the Buffalo, even though his business sits right on the White River. Now, he estimates his business on the Buffalo may be one percent. According to Charles, "Park rangers are constantly monitoring every boat for liquor, and if you camp out, they stop and check you. You might say the soul has been taken out of the Buffalo River experience."

A few years after Joe Bennett, the previous owner of Bennett's Canoe Rental, sold his canoe business, he went fishing at Carver and took a friend. No one was there. It was peaceful and quiet. They were minding their own business, enjoying the tranquility, when all of a sudden a park ranger showed up and started talking to them. They were friendly and respectful to him. The next thing Joe knew the ranger was looking in a cooler Joe had in his truck. He'd stopped at a store and happened to find some Orange Crush in glass bottles. The ranger told Joe he was going to have to ticket him for having glass bottles. Joe was not happy, but he didn't say much, understanding no glass bottles are allowed, and "rules are rules," he said.

Then, the ranger started looking under Joe's truck seat, then behind the seat, digging through everything he could find. Joe got furious and went over to the park ranger's truck and started doing the same thing, digging around in the ranger's stuff. The ranger threatened to arrest Joe, until he told the park ranger that he was a former canoe operator, and was friends with Jack Linehan, Superintendent of the Park Service headquartered in Harrison. Suddenly, the ranger changed his tune, became respectful, and left Joe alone to fish and enjoy the peace of the Buffalo.

Joe Bennett doesn't believe the NPS has improved the river experience or the plight of the canoe operator. He says when he left, the Park Service was collecting a fee of 2 percent of his gross collections; it increased to 7 percent. He doesn't believe people are flocking to the river like they did in the past. Some big groups, such as church groups, that used to come yearly don't seem to come as often.

Park rangers are even staging watches in bushes in unexpected places between Highway 14 Bridge and Rush and then arresting the floaters later when they get to their take-out place. Joe tells of a friend who was camping at Buffalo Point with young children. A copperhead snake was seen crawling close to their picnic table. The guy killed the snake and later when a park ranger came by and saw the dead snake, he wrote the dad a ticket for killing a copperhead. Similarly, he knew someone who was given a ticket for skipping a rock across the river. The park ranger wrote the person a ticket for defacing government property. "People don't come to the river to be hassled; they come to get away and be free," Joe said.

Today, Bill Scruggs, who owns "Wild Bill's Outfitters," (originally Barnes Canoe Rental), the largest canoe service on the Buffalo, says he appreciates the NPS and that the regulations are mostly things he'd do anyway, such as keeping insurance and the upkeep of his vehicles. One of the main complaints he has heard regarding the NPS is the way they manage access roads to the river. These are the old roads that access cemeteries and pieces of land that might not be accessible any way other than through an NPS road. He has heard of people not being able to visit cemeteries where their relatives are buried.

Bill says if he has a problem with a regulation, he just goes and talks to the superintendent. For example, for a while the Park Service would not allow stacking up canoes at access points, like the Highway 14 Bridge or Maumee. "There's no way we could function without having canoes there," Bill said. He explained the problem to someone at the NPS and they found a way to amend that regulation and make it work for him.

A few years ago, Robert Baysinger, who used to guide for Joe Barnes and lives close to the river, bought eighty acres of wilderness land. There was only one access road to this piece of property. The NPS had the access road blocked with large rocks, and told Robert he couldn't use it. After he hired a lawyer, Robert took the necessary steps to gain access to his land. He soon had an easement across the road to his land. He moved the big rocks, built a gate, and put a lock on it. Then, the NPS ended up asking for a key to Robert's lock on the gate, which he eventually gave them.

Another often heard complaint against the NPS is the attitude of some of the park rangers. Not all, just some. Some time ago, my sister Justine was driving down the Buffalo River hill almost to the Highway 14 Bridge on her way home. She saw a few rocks on the side of the hill and decided to stop and pick them up for her flower bed. She pulled over, got out of her car, walked down Highway 14 a few yards, picked up a couple of rocks, and started walking back to her car. The next thing she knew Jeff West, a park ranger, had pulled over behind her and parked. He got out of his truck and said, "Lady...hey, lady...what are you doing?"

"Just picking up a couple rocks for my flower bed," she answered.

"Lady, you can't do that; this is government property."

She threw the rocks down and slowly walked back to her car. As soon as the ranger had driven out of sight, she got out, picked up the same rocks, and put them inside the car, on the floorboard.

One question often heard regarding the NPS management of the Buffalo is have they protected what they were given stewardship of forty-two years ago? According to some who live in Searcy County, when the NPS took over, there were no major areas of erosion from Woolum to Gilbert. Now, there is major erosion occurring below Woolum, Goggen's Ford, Rye Bottom, Peter Cave Shoal, Baker's Ford, Arnold Ford, Calf Creek confluence, Tyler Bend, Grinders Ferry, Goat Bluff, Judge Moore Spring, and Hubbard Crossing. It's believed by some that the NPS has done nothing to stop the erosion and wasting in these areas; as a result, many acres of ancient lands have washed from Searcy County to White River, to the Arkansas River, to the Mississippi River—all the way to the Gulf of Mexico. Others say this might not have occurred if it hadn't been for earlier massive land clearing, bulldozing, and cattle operations. Yes, this may be the way nature has allowed the course of the Buffalo to take since then. But isn't the real question, what has the NPS done to stop it? Was this their responsibility once the Buffalo was made a national river?

The NPS's answer to the erosion problem goes something like this: "It's the way nature would define the course of the Buffalo." For this reason, they have done nothing. Could they initiate a plan to stop or slow the current erosion as they have united to stop or restrict the hog farming? Should they consult with local county agents and soil conservation districts? Could they consider suggestions from adjacent land owners?

"It just kills me to go down to the bridge and look at the river and see the way the channel has widened and how shallow the water is. It breaks my heart," said Shirley Huddleston, who once lived on South Highway 14. Landowners would never have tolerated some of these erosion losses. Some people say that when landowners govern their own land, there's an ebb and flow to the changes. They will protect and treasure what they own. For years the landowners along the Buffalo managed it, some better than others. Some would clear cut timber. Others would hunt and kill game illegally, leaving the next generation less timber and game. But somehow, the next generation after that would have timber and game once again. The game situation has been improved significantly through effective management by the Arkansas Game and Fish Commission.

If the river flooded and brush and trees piled up in an area preventing the river from flowing, a landowner knew how to unplug it by burning it out when the river was low, or whatever way he could manage. Farmers and landowners say the best thing for the health of the river is just to leave it alone and give it the freedom— the freedom to ebb and flow.

To illustrate this concept, once at Buffalo Point after a flood, the river had washed away the dirt road that circled down and around the parking area. This section of road is closer to the river, which makes it easier to carry a canoe from the river up the hill and load on a truck or a trailer. The river rarely floods up that high but when it does, it washes away whatever is there.

After this one particular flood the NPS decided to replace the dirt road with a paved road. Joe Barnes told them, "Boys, you might as well use some clay dirt and gravel for this road. Be cheaper and won't matter if it's washed away. The river will wash away whatever is there." Nonetheless, NPS went ahead and put in the paved road. It wasn't long until another flood came and washed it out. The rumor was that paved road had cost around $200,000.00. Now, instead of fixing the road, they've done nothing since the last time it washed out a few years ago. They have some road-blocking sawhorses and no one can drive down there. People have to carry their canoes or kayaks and equipment all the way up the hill. Instead of having a beautiful, convenient place to stop and take out of the river, huge, orange plastic road dividers now block the remaining road damage.

Yes, the Buffalo has been a majestic throne to many of us; a throne where it's clear that we are a part of something much bigger than ourselves. It is a good place where people can come to grips with their own insignificance and vulnerability. The river can have that effect on people. The peace and stillness that the river brings is priceless. Who knows best how to preserve that? Landowners? The National Park Service?

Story after story can be heard from local folks all up and down the Buffalo. Maybe someone will collect more of those stories and write them down. What if we have a pristine river and perfect trails and no glass bottles? What if someone is peering over our shoulder all the time? What if the soul of the river experience is gradually lost and forgotten? What do we lose with the loss of these liberties? Surely, there can be an effective balance found.

Here's one liberty almost lost. My father passed away in 2005. His four daughters decided it would be fitting to have his funeral at one of the pavilions at Buffalo Point. It seemed like a logical place, considering Joe had helped build the park when he was in the CCC, he married Willodean on the road between Pavillion #1 and the main swimming area, he'd owned the largest canoe business on the Buffalo, and he'd been an upstanding member of the South Highway 14 community. When the Park Service was approached about this and permission was requested to use the pavilion, they denied it. There was some regulation against using government property for private ceremonies. Then, Doretha Shipman called the NPS and suggested that since her father, Pate Dillard, donated that property to the state for park use, it would be good if they offered the pavilion for the funeral of Joe Barnes, her friend and relative. They acquiesced.

Genealogy

JOE AND WILLODEAN BARNES

Joseph William Barnes (3/16/1919–4/16/2005)
Mary Willodean Smith Barnes (1/22/1918 –11/21/2004)
They were married 4/7/1941 halfway down the big hill going down
to the Buffalo River, close to what is now known as Buffalo Point.

Children of Joe and Bill:
Shirley Jo Barnes Huddleston (3/5/1942–   )
Virginia (Jenny) Leah Barnes Butler (11/6/1946–   )
Justine Barnes France (8/23/1949–   )
Scarlett Dean Barnes Fagan (1/17/1960–   )

JOE BARNES'S PARENTS AND SIBLINGS

Joseph George Barnes (1882–11/8/1950)
Rena Bowers Finch [adopted name] Barnes (2/14/1887–3/7/1980)
They were married in 12/3/1911. Both were born in Independence
County, Magness, Arkansas

Children of Rena and Joseph George:
Margurite (9/2/1912–12/3/1912
George D (8/13/19–2/13/1915)
James Lindsey (2/11/1916–unknown)
Joseph William (3/16/1919–4/16/2005)
Jarrell Franklin (1/14/1921–unknown)
Baby never named (1/8/1923–1/8/1923)
Jorden Robert (12/29/1923–1/27/2006)
Kenneth Kirby (7/14/1927–9/24/1999)

MARY WILLODEAN SMITH BARNES'S PARENTS AND SIBLINGS

Benjamin Harrison Smith and Alice Idella Dillard

Children of Harrison and Alice:
Jessie Willard (4/15/1915 –8/10/1967)
Mary Willodean [twin] (1/22/1918–11/24/2004)
Evelyn [twin] (1/22/1918–unknown)
Bennie (10/31/1922–unknown)
LeeRoy (6/17/1926–)
Billy Frank (1/27/1931–)
Mary Elizabeth (5/29/1949–)
Sammie Lane [twin] (2/19/1936–)
Kenneth [twin] (2/19/1936–)
Patty Jo [granddaughter] (1/31/1938–)

MATERNAL GRANDPARENTS OF MARY WILLODEAN SMITH BARNES

James Franklin "Doc" Dillard and Nancy Elizabeth "Lizzie" Smith Dillard. Lizzie is the daughter of William Lenard and Mary Ellen Smith. Doc is the son of Mary Magdalene "Mandy" Dillard.

Children of Doc and Lizzie:
Arthur William Dillard (9/7/1882–9/29/1972)
Osker Dillard (1/22/1884– 12/1893)
Guy Anderson Dillard (6/14/1886– 5/14/1968)
Mabel Violet Dillard (3/10/1889–6/22/1973)
Clarence D. Dillard (8/2/1893–10/1/1969)
Pate Dillard (8/22/1893–6/6/1985)
Leroy Dillard [twin] (12/23/1894–9/13/1929)
Ira D. Dillard [twin] (12/23/1894–9/13/1929)
Alice Idella Dillard (2/22/1897–1/25/1985)
Mary Demoia Dillard (1900–1910)
Rosa Dillard (1902–1990)
Ora Bazze Dillard (8/15/1904–2/29/1968)
James Frank Dillard (10/24/1907–12/6/1970)
Theodore Roosevelt "Ted" Dillard (3/24/1912–3/28/1968)

PATERNAL GRANDPARENTS OF MARY WILLODEAN SMITH BARNES

William Thomas Marion Smith and Mary Missouri Carolina Moody Smith

Children of Thomas and Mary:

Wyley (unknown–unknown)
John William (accidentally shot himself around "three")
Anna (died of typhoid 2 days later)
Ora
James Franklin
Benjamin Harrison (1888–1948)
Audie Calvin
Ancil Jewel
Arthur Seran
Monty Floyd
Columbus
Iona Inez

GREAT GRANDMOTHER OF MARY WILLODEAN SMITH BARNES

Mary Magdalene "Mandy" Dillard
Mary settled near Dill Spring at Freck in Searcy County, Arkansas.
She is listed in the 1860 census in the household of David and Silena household with four of her children.

Children of Mandy:

Julia (1852–1942)
Margaret Josephine (1854–1894)
Elmira E. (1856–1922)
James Franklin "Doc" (1859–1935)
Harriet (1863–1923)
John Pickney (1867–1914)
Margaret Salina (1869–1953)
William "Bill" (1872–1957)

Acknowledgments

This book started as little scenes popping up in my mind. I remembered Joe "gut giggling" about his three-year-old grandson, Matt, licking a toothless woman's ice cream. I could see my mother getting on the school bus with an empty stomach. I froze in my tracks one day when I realized my Grandmother Rena lost two babies in infancy before she had a child thrive. I determined to write some of these things down and add pictures so the grandkids would know their heritage. I wanted them to know that hard times can breed good things, and that an easy, good life is not handed to many.

After my father's death, my sisters and I learned more and more stories about him. Many places we went, people would tell us something Joe or Willodean had said or done. Larry Davenport, at the Buffalo Point Dining Room, often mentioned, "I miss ole Joe; he was real." Gordon Davenport told me a few weeks ago, "You could count on Joe to tell you the truth." Wow! What a heritage. "He won't die," my sisters and I say to each other.

Thank you to Jerry Patterson from Marshall, who told me early in my investigation of all that happened with the prospectus meetings, "This is a story that has never been told." I thought "really?" I'm a reader; not a writer! I don't want to do this. Then, my sister Shirley talked to Scotty Jefferson, who had just had a long visit with Robert Baysinger. Shirley insisted she and I go visit Robert and interview him. I wrote down every word he said. Robert was a grand historian and he remembered dates and details and significant events. Most of all, he cherished his friendship with Joe. "Joe was my friend," he said. Robert answered every question and every phone call.

Thank you to Joe Bennett who was young when he started coming to the Buffalo with his family and young when he started his canoe business. Joe fearlessly recalled stories of his life along the river, his opinion of what is going on now, and his memory of sad stories on the river.

Charles Newland actually found the reel-to-reel tapes he'd made of the prospectus meetings. Thank you, Charles, for your insight into the past and how it compares to the present.

Thank you to Mike Mills. Stan and I met Mike for the first time when we went to Ponca to float a few years back. When I told Mike I was Joe Barnes's daughter, he was warm and friendly. The first thing Mike did was cock his cap to the right and say, "Why, hell yes!" as Joe would say it. Then, Mike showed us his scrapbook with all of the newspaper articles of the prospectus meetings. He pointed out pictures of Joe. He said, "Joe was my mentor." That meeting was probably the first inkling I had of the positive impact Joe Barnes had on some folks.

Many others encouraged me at times when I was ready to throw in the towel. Thanks to Carol Lester for her prayers, and for her friendship. Thanks to Lou Strain for her enthusiasm and insight. Thanks to Andrea Self for caring and for being my friend, even though she is "young." Thank you to Janet Parsch for encouragement at a critical time and for her honesty. Thank you to Raymond Lynch for his time and willingness to tell his thoughts about Joe and Willodean.

A special thanks to Scotty Jefferson for his response after he read the manuscript before it was finished. I cried, and told my husband, "Maybe this project will be worth the seven years we've put into it."

Thank you to Rita Robinson for teaching me we can do more and are more gifted and talented than we think. What a writer she is!

Thank you to many others who have been tolerant of my questions and then more questions.

Thank you to my husband, Stan Butler, for all the times he tiptoed quietly around in the mornings so I could think and write. Who could ask for a better man to share one's life? Not I.